MASTER THE™ DSST®

General Anthropology Exam

About Peterson's

Peterson's® has been your trusted educational publisher for over 50 years. It's a milestone we're quite proud of, as we continue to offer the most accurate, dependable, high-quality educational content in the field, providing you with everything you need to succeed. No matter where you are on your academic or professional path, you can rely on Peterson's for its books, online information, expert test-prep tools, the most up-to-date education exploration data, and the highest quality career success resources—everything you need to achieve your education goals. For our complete line of products, visit www.petersons.com.

For more information, contact Peterson's, 8740 Lucent Blvd., Suite 400, Highlands Ranch, CO 80129; 800-338-3282 Ext. 54229; or find us online at **www.petersons.com**.

ISBN: 978-0-7689-4452-5

Printed in the United States of America

10 9 8 7 6 5 4 3 2 1   22 21 20

Contents

Before You Begin

HOW THIS BOOK IS ORGANIZED

Peterson's *Master the*™ *DSST® General Anthropology Exam* provides a diagnostic test, subject-matter review, and a post-test.

- **Diagnostic Test**—Twenty multiple-choice questions, followed by an answer key with detailed answer explanations
- **Assessment Grid**—A chart designed to help you identify areas that you need to focus on based on your test results
- **Subject-Matter Review**—General overview of the exam subject, followed by a review of the relevant topics and terminology covered on the exam
- **Post-test**—Sixty multiple-choice questions, followed by an answer key and detailed answer explanations

The purpose of the diagnostic test is to help you figure out what you know—or don't know. The twenty multiple-choice questions are similar to the ones found on the DSST exam, and they should provide you with a good idea of what to expect. Once you take the diagnostic test, check your answers to see how you did. Included with each correct answer is a brief explanation regarding why a specific answer is correct, and in many cases, why other options are incorrect. Use the assessment grid to identify the questions you miss so that you can spend more time reviewing that information later. As with any exam, knowing your weak spots greatly improves your chances of success.

Following the diagnostic test is a subject-matter review. The review summarizes the various topics covered on the DSST exam. Key terms are defined; important concepts are explained; and when appropriate, examples are provided. As you read the review, some of the information may seem familiar while other information may seem foreign. Again, take note of the unfamiliar because that will most likely cause you problems on the actual exam.

After studying the subject-matter review, you should be ready for the post-test. The post-test contains sixty multiple-choice items, and it will serve as a dry run for the real DSST exam. There are complete answer explanations at the end of the test.

OTHER DSST® PRODUCTS BY PETERSON'S

Books, flashcards, practice tests, and videos available online at **www.petersons.com/testprep/dsst**

- Art of the Western World
- Astronomy
- Business Mathematics
- Business Ethics and Society
- Civil War and Reconstruction
- Computing and Information Technology
- Criminal Justice
- Environmental Science
- Ethics in America
- Ethics in Technology
- Foundations of Education
- Fundamentals of College Algebra
- Fundamentals of Counseling
- Fundamentals of Cybersecurity
- General Anthropology
- Health and Human Development
- History of the Soviet Union
- History of the Vietnam War
- Human Resource Management
- Introduction to Business
- Introduction to Geography
- Introduction to Geology
- Introduction to Law Enforcement
- Introduction to World Religions
- Lifespan Developmental Psychology
- Math for Liberal Arts
- Management Information Systems
- Money and Banking
- Organizational Behavior
- Personal Finance
- Principles of Advanced English Composition
- Principles of Finance
- Principles of Public Speaking
- Principles of Statistics
- Principles of Supervision
- Substance Abuse
- Technical Writing

Like what you see? Get unlimited access to Peterson's full catalog of DSST practice tests, instructional videos, flashcards and more for **75% off the first month**! Go to **www.petersons.com/testprep/dsst** and use coupon code **DSST2020** at checkout. Offer expires July 1, 2021.

Chapter 1

All About the DSST® Exam

WHAT IS DSST®?

Previously known as the DANTES Subject Standardized Tests, the DSST program provides the opportunity for individuals to earn college credit for what they have learned outside of the traditional classroom. Accepted or administered at more than 1,900 colleges and universities nationwide and approved by the American Council on Education (ACE), the DSST program enables individuals to use the knowledge they have acquired outside the classroom to accomplish their educational and professional goals.

WHY TAKE A DSST® EXAM?

DSST exams offer a way for you to save both time and money in your quest for a college education. Why enroll in a college course in a subject you already understand? For more than 30 years, the DSST program has offered the perfect solution for individuals who are knowledgeable in a specific subject and want to save both time and money. A passing score on a DSST exam provides physical evidence to universities of proficiency in a specific subject. More than 1,900 accredited and respected colleges and universities across the nation award undergraduate credit for passing scores on DSST exams. With the DSST program, individuals can shave months off the time it takes to earn a degree.

The DSST program offers numerous advantages for individuals in all stages of their educational development:

- Adult learners
- College students
- Military personnel

Adult learners desiring college degrees face unique circumstances—demanding work schedules, family responsibilities, and tight budgets. Yet adult learners also have years of valuable work experience that can frequently be applied toward a degree through the DSST program. For example, adult learners with on-the-job experience in business and management might be able to skip the Business 101 courses if they earn passing marks on DSST exams such as Introduction to Business and Principles of Supervision.

Adult learners can put their prior learning into action and move forward with more advanced course work. Adults who have never enrolled in a college course may feel a little uncertain about their abilities. If this describes your situation, then sign up for a DSST exam and see how you do. A passing score may be the boost you need to realize your dream of earning a degree. With family and work commitments, adult learners often feel they lack the time to attend college. The DSST program provides adult learners with the unique opportunity to work toward college degrees without the time constraints of semester-long course work. DSST exams take two hours or less to complete. In one weekend, you could earn credit for multiple college courses.

The DSST exams also benefit students who are already enrolled in a college or university. With college tuition costs on the rise, most students face financial challenges. The fee for each DSST exam starts at $80 (plus administration fees charged by some testing facilities)—significantly less than the $750 average cost of a 3-hour college class. Maximize tuition assistance by taking DSST exams for introductory or mandatory course work. Once you earn a passing score on a DSST exam, you are free to move on to higher-level course work in that subject matter, take desired electives, or focus on courses in a chosen major.

Not only do college students and adult learners profit from DSST exams, but military personnel reap the benefits as well. If you are a member of the armed services at home or abroad, you can initiate your post-military career by taking DSST exams in areas with which you have experience. Military personnel can gain credit anywhere in the world, thanks to the fact that almost all of the tests are available through the internet at designated testing locations. DSST testing facilities are located at more than 500 military installations, so service members on active duty can get a jump-start on a post-military career with the DSST program. As an additional incentive, DANTES (Defense Activity for Non-Traditional Education Support) provides funding for DSST test fees for eligible members of the military.

More than 30 subject-matter tests are available in the fields of Business, Humanities, Math, Physical Science, Social Sciences, and Technology.

Available DSST® Exams

Business	Social Sciences
Business Ethics and Society	A History of the Vietnam War
Business Mathematics	Art of the Western World
Computing and Information Technology	Criminal Justice
Human Resource Management	Foundations of Education
Introduction to Business	Fundamentals of Counseling
Management Information Systems	General Anthropology
Money and Banking	History of the Soviet Union
Organizational Behavior	Introduction to Geography
Personal Finance	Introduction to Law Enforcement
Principles of Finance	Lifespan Developmental Psychology
Principles of Supervision	Substance Abuse
	The Civil War and Reconstruction
Humanities	**Physical Sciences**
Ethics in America	Astronomy
Introduction to World Religions	Environment Science
Principles of Advanced English	Health and Human Development
Composition	Introduction to Geology
Principles of Public Speaking	
Math	**Technology**
Fundamentals of College Algebra	Ethics in Technology
Math for Liberal Arts	Fundamentals of Cybersecurity
Principles of Statistics	Technical Writing

As you can see from the table, the DSST program covers a wide variety of subjects. However, it is important to ask two questions before registering for a DSST exam.

1. Which universities or colleges award credit for passing DSST exams?
2. Which DSST exams are the most relevant to my desired degree and my experience?

Knowing which universities offer DSST credit is important. In all likelihood, a college in your area awards credit for DSST exams, but find out before taking an exam by contacting the university directly. Then review the list of DSST exams to determine which ones are most relevant to the degree you are seeking and to your base of knowledge. Schedule an appointment with your college adviser to determine which exams best fit your degree program and which college courses the DSST exams can replace. Advisers should also be able to tell you the minimum score required on the DSST exam to receive university credit.

DSST® TEST CENTERS

You can find DSST testing locations in community colleges and universities across the country. Check the DSST website (**www.getcollegecredit. com**) for a location near you or contact your local college or university to find out if the school administers DSST exams. Keep in mind that some universities and colleges administer DSST exams only to enrolled students. DSST testing is available to men and women in the armed services at more than 500 military installations around the world.

HOW TO REGISTER FOR A DSST® EXAM

Once you have located a nearby DSST testing facility, you need to contact the testing center to find out the exam administration schedule. Many centers are set up to administer tests via the internet, while others use printed materials. Almost all DSST exams are available as online tests, but the method used depends on the testing center. The cost for each DSST exam starts at $80, and many testing locations charge a fee to cover their costs for administering the tests. Credit cards are the only accepted payment method for taking online DSST exams. Credit card, certified check, and money order are acceptable payment methods for paper-and-pencil tests.

Test takers are allotted two score reports—one mailed to them and another mailed to a designated college or university, if requested. Online tests generate unofficial scores at the end of the test session, while individuals taking paper tests must wait four to six weeks for score reports.

PREPARING FOR A DSST® EXAM

Even though you are knowledgeable in a certain subject matter, you should still prepare for the test to ensure you achieve the highest score possible. The first step in studying for a DSST exam is to find out what will be on the specific test you have chosen. Information regarding test content is located on the DSST fact sheets, which can be downloaded at no cost from **www.getcollegecredit.com**. Each fact sheet outlines the topics covered on a subject-matter test, as well as the approximate percentage assigned to each topic. For example, questions on the General Anthropology exam are distributed in the following way: Anthropology: Methodologies and Disciplines—8%, History and Theory—11%, Physical Anthropology—13%, Archaeology—10%, Cultural Systems and Processes—14%, Social Organization—10%, Economic and Political Organization—11%, Religion—11%, and Modernization and Application—12%.

In addition to the breakdown of topics on a DSST exam, the fact sheet also lists recommended reference materials. If you do not own the recommended books, then check college bookstores. Avoid paying high prices for new textbooks by looking online for used textbooks. Don't panic if you are unable to locate a specific textbook listed on the fact sheet; the textbooks are merely recommendations. Instead, search for comparable books used in university courses on the specific subject. Current editions are ideal, and it is a good idea to use at least two references when studying for a DSST exam. Of course, the subject matter provided in this book will be a sufficient review for most test takers. However, if you need additional information, then it is a good idea to have some of the reference materials at your disposal when preparing for a DSST exam.

Fact sheets include other useful information in addition to a list of reference materials and topics. Each fact sheet includes subject-specific sample questions like those you will encounter on the DSST exam. The sample questions provide an idea of the types of questions you can expect on the exam. Test questions are multiple-choice with one correct answer and three incorrect choices.

The fact sheet also includes information about the number of credit hours ACE has recommended be awarded by colleges for a passing DSST exam score. However, you should keep in mind that not all universities and colleges adhere to the ACE recommendation for DSST credit hours. Some institutions require DSST exam scores higher than the minimum score recommended by ACE. Once you have acquired appropriate reference materials and you have the outline provided on the fact sheet, you are ready to start studying, which is where this book can help.

TEST DAY

After reviewing the material and taking practice tests, you are finally ready to take your DSST exam. Follow these tips for a successful test day experience.

1. **Arrive on time.** Not only is it courteous to arrive on time to the DSST testing facility, but it also allows plenty of time for you to take care of check-in procedures and settle into your surroundings.

2. **Bring identification.** DSST test facilities require that candidates bring a valid government-issued identification card with a current photo and signature. Acceptable forms of identification include a current driver's license, passport, military identification card, or state-issued identification card. Individuals who fail to bring proper identification to the DSST testing facility will not be allowed to take an exam.

3. **Bring the right supplies.** If your exam requires the use of a calculator, you may bring a calculator that meets the specifications. For paper-based exams, you may also bring No. 2 pencils with an eraser and black ballpoint pens. Regardless of the exam methodology, you are NOT allowed to bring reference or study materials, scratch paper, or electronics such as cell phones, personal handheld devices, cameras, alarm wrist watches, or tape recorders to the testing center.

4. **Take the test.** During the exam, take the time to read each question-and-answer option carefully. Eliminate the choices you know are incorrect to narrow the number of potential answers. If a question completely stumps you, take an educated guess and move on—remember that DSSTs are timed; you will have 2 hours to take the exam.

With the proper preparation, DSST exams will save you both time and money. So join the thousands of people who have already reaped the benefits of DSST exams and move closer than ever to your college degree.

GENERAL ANTHROPOLOGY EXAM FACTS

The DSST® General Anthropology exam consists of 100 multiple-choice that cover the four fields of anthropology: physical anthropology, archaeology, cultural anthropology, and linguistic anthropology. The exam focuses upon the following topics: methodologies and disciplines; cultural systems and processes; history and theory; social organization; economic and political organization; religion; and the modernization and application of anthropology. Careful reading, critical thinking, and logical analysis will be as important as your anthropological knowledge.

Area or Course Equivalent: General Anthropology
Level: Lower-level baccalaureate
Amount of Credit: 3 Semester Hours
Minimum Score: 400
Source: https://www.getcollegecredit.com/wp-content/assets/factsheets
/GeneralAnthropology.pdf

Below is an outline of what you can expect to be covered on the exam.

I. Anthropology: Methodologies and Disciplines – 8%

   a. Physical anthropology

   b. Cultural Anthropology

   c. Linguistics

   d. Archaeology

   e. Applied anthropology

II. History and Theory – 11%

   a. Ethnographies and perspectives

   b. Sex and Gender

   c. Race and ethnicity

   d. Cultural ecology and evolution

III. Physical Anthropology – 13%

   a. Genetic principles

   b. Evolutionary principles

   c. Primatology

   d. Paleontology

     1. Relative and absolute dating

     2. Fossil hominids

IV. Archaeology – 10%

   a. Methodology

   b. Paleolithic and Mesolithic

   c. Neolithic

   d. Development of civilization and urban societies

V. Cultural Systems and Processes – 14%

   a. Components of culture

b. Symbolic Systems

c. Language and communication

d. Cultural diffusion and power

e. Cultural universals, sub-cultures and counter cultures

f. World system and colonialism

g. Arts

VI. Social Organization – 10%

a. Marriage and family patterns

b. Kinship and descent groups

c. Social and economic stratification

VII. Economic and Political Organization – 11%

a. Bands, tribes, chiefdoms, and states

b. Subsistence and settlement patterns

c. Trade, reciprocity, redistribution, and market exchange

d. Modern political systems

e. Globalization and the Environment

VIII. Religion – 11%

a. Belief Systems

b. Formal institutions

c. Informal organizations

d. Religious practices and practitioners

e. Rituals

IX. Modernization and Application – 12%

a. Applied anthropology

b. Cultural preservation

c. Directed and spontaneous cultural change

d. Future Directions

1. Environment

2. Cultural resource management

3. Indigenous survival and global culture

Chapter 2

General Anthropology Diagnostic Test

DIAGNOSTIC TEST ANSWER SHEET

1. Ⓐ Ⓑ Ⓒ Ⓓ
2. Ⓐ Ⓑ Ⓒ Ⓓ
3. Ⓐ Ⓑ Ⓒ Ⓓ
4. Ⓐ Ⓑ Ⓒ Ⓓ
5. Ⓐ Ⓑ Ⓒ Ⓓ
6. Ⓐ Ⓑ Ⓒ Ⓓ
7. Ⓐ Ⓑ Ⓒ Ⓓ

8. Ⓐ Ⓑ Ⓒ Ⓓ
9. Ⓐ Ⓑ Ⓒ Ⓓ
10. Ⓐ Ⓑ Ⓒ Ⓓ
11. Ⓐ Ⓑ Ⓒ Ⓓ
12. Ⓐ Ⓑ Ⓒ Ⓓ
13. Ⓐ Ⓑ Ⓒ Ⓓ
14. Ⓐ Ⓑ Ⓒ Ⓓ

15. Ⓐ Ⓑ Ⓒ Ⓓ
16. Ⓐ Ⓑ Ⓒ Ⓓ
17. Ⓐ Ⓑ Ⓒ Ⓓ
18. Ⓐ Ⓑ Ⓒ Ⓓ
19. Ⓐ Ⓑ Ⓒ Ⓓ
20. Ⓐ Ⓑ Ⓒ Ⓓ

GENERAL ANTHROPOLOGY DIAGNOSTIC TEST

Directions: Carefully read each of the following 20 questions. Choose the best answer to each question and fill in the corresponding circle on the answer sheet. The Answer Key and Explanations can be found following this Diagnostic Test.

1. Anthropology traditionally includes which four subdisciplines?

    A. Physical anthropology, archaeology, ethnobotany, and cultural anthropology

    B. Cultural anthropology, physical anthropology, anthropological linguistics, paleontology

    C. Anthropological linguistics, physical anthropology, archaeology, and economics

    D. Cultural anthropology, linguistic anthropology, archaeology, and physical anthropology

2. Absolute dating of a fossil is important to paleoanthropologists because

    A. fossils disintegrate quickly.

    B. the age of human bones can only be tested with absolute dating methods.

    C. it helps them more accurately reconstruct the timeline of human evolution.

    D. relative dating methods are accurate for anything younger than 100 years old.

3. What is the difference between innovation and invention?

    A. Innovation refers to an improvement or change to something that already exists. Invention refers to the development or discovery of something completely new.

    B. Invention refers to an improvement or change to something that already exists. Innovation refers to the development or discovery of something completely new.

    C. Invention and innovation both refer to the improvements made to existing products or services.

    D. Innovation and invention both refer to the development of a new product or service.

4. Tribal political organizations are usually found in which type of society?

A. Pastoralists
B. Agriculturalist
C. Band
D. Foraging

5. What is applied anthropology?

A. Using an anthropological perspective to solve modern problems
B. An anthropological technique that started in the 1980s
C. Anthropologists working with paleontologists digging for dinosaurs
D. An anthropological study of employment

6. Anthropologists say that agriculture is a necessary precursor to the development of urban society because

A. human societies evolve through the same stages.
B. intensive food production is required to feed large populations
C. humans finally had time to develop tools.
D. writing allowed people to share farming techniques with one another.

7. What is the primary difference between historic archaeologists and prehistoric archaeologists?

A. Prehistoric archaeologists are interested in terrestrial research sites, while historic archaeologists are interested in underwater research sites.
B. Prehistoric archaeologists are interested in human culture prior to the advent of written records, while historic archaeologists are interested in human cultures who used some form of writing.
C. Prehistoric archaeologists are interested in artifacts, while historic archaeologists are interested in written documents.
D. Prehistoric archaeologists are interested in dinosaurs, while historic archaeologists are interested in modern humans.

8. Bronislaw Malinowski proposed his theory of Functionalism after years of conducting fieldwork where?

A. The Philippines
B. The Trobriand Islands
C. The Marshall Islands
D. The island of Malta

9. From an anthropological perspective, what is an age group?

A. People of the same age who share common interests
B. A kinship term
C. A survey category
D. People of the same age who experience culturally relevant experiences at the same time

10. Which anthropologists could use their skills to develop programs to help multilingual students succeed in school?

A. Physical anthropologists
B. Structural linguists
C. Historic archaeologists
D. Sociolinguists

11. What are random changes in DNA that may lead to beneficial, harmful, or neutral traits for an organism?

A. Genetic drift
B. Gene flow
C. Mutation
D. Phenotype

12. Which anthropologist would be most likely to research the translation of writing on a stone table?

A. Primatologist
B. Historic archaeologist
C. Forensic anthropologist
D. Physical anthropologist

13. What is the name of the theory that states cultural institutions function to fulfill basic human biological needs and support the workings of society?

    A. Functionalism
    B. Anthropology and Gender
    C. Postmodernism
    D. Globalization

14. "People shouldn't eat fried grasshoppers for protein because that's gross and unnatural. Meat is the only protein people should eat." This statement is an example of what perspective?

    A. Ethnocentric perspective
    B. Holistic perspective
    C. Four-field perspective
    D. Culturally relative perspective

15. What is a gene pool?

    A. A laboratory sample of an individual's DNA
    B. All of the possible genetic variations within the human species
    C. The product of a sperm fertilizing an egg
    D. The visible traits of a population

16. Rituals that mark an individual's movement from one social status or stage of life to another are

    A. rites of witchcraft
    B. rites of intensification
    C. rites of passage
    D. rites of purification

17. Enculturation of the individual happens

    A. at birth.
    B. during childhood.
    C. as a teenager becomes an adult.
    D. throughout a person's entire life.

18. Which statement best describes the incest taboo from an anthropological perspective?

A. The prohibitions of an incest taboo differ between cultures.
B. The incest taboo is one of the four forces of evolution.
C. Societies prefer monogamous marriages to avoid incest.
D. The prohibitions of an incest taboo are the same between cultures.

19. Pastoralism is a subsistence strategy that relies on which of the following for survival?

A. Long-term breeding of livestock
B. Large territories for agriculture
C. Caring for and keeping herds of domesticated animals
D. Communal gardens

20. A shaman is a

A. priestess.
B. healer.
C. totem.
D. pilgrim.

ANSWER KEY AND EXPLANATIONS

1. D	**5.** A	**9.** D	**13.** A	**17.** D
2. C	**6.** B	**10.** D	**14.** A	**18.** A
3. A	**7.** B	**11.** C	**15.** B	**19.** C
4. A	**8.** B	**12.** B	**16.** C	**20.** B

1. **The correct answer is D.** Anthropology studies the entirety of the human experience: the biological history and diversity of humanity (physical anthropology); the study of prehistoric and historic human cultures based on their material remains (archaeology); the study of human language (linguistic anthropology); and human cultural diversity (cultural anthropology). Choice A is incorrect because ethnobotany is the study of the relationship between plant life and humans. Choice B is incorrect because paleontology is the study of life on earth prior to the emergence of anatomically modern human beings. Choice C is incorrect because economics studies human decision-making regarding goods and services.

2. **The correct answer is C.** Since paleoanthropologists have identified many possible relatives of *Homo sapiens*, an accurate age of the fossils could help them determine when these other groups were alive on earth. It would then be easier to reconstruct the evolutionary changes that occurred over time. Choice A is incorrect because fossils are usually preserved as rock. Choice B is incorrect because the age of human bones can be determined through stratigraphy, an example of a relative dating method. Choice D is incorrect because relative dating methods can date fossils to millions of years ago.

3. **The correct answer is A.** The difference between invention and innovation is important. *Invention* refers to the development or discovery of something completely new. This may refer to a new idea, product, service, tool, etc. *Innovation* refers to an improvement or change to something that already exists—that is, something that has already been invented. Choice B is incorrect because the definition is mismatched to the words. Choices C and D are incorrect because the words are not synonyms.

4. **The correct answer is A.** A tribe, which is usually found in pastoralist or horticulturalist cultures, is made up of groups related by kinship or family ties. Choice B is incorrect because agriculturalists usually organize themselves through a state system. Choices C and D are incorrect because foragers are usually organized into bands.

5. **The correct answer is A.** Applied anthropology uses the perspective and tools of physical, archaeological, linguistic, and cultural anthropology to solve a variety of problems. Choice B is incorrect because applied anthropology dates to the early 1940s. Choice C is incorrect because anthropologists do not excavate sites for dinosaurs. Choice D is incorrect because applied anthropology does not refer to an ethnographic study.

6. **The correct answer is B.** Agriculture allowed people to settle in one place and, over time, begin growing enough food to sustain larger and larger populations. Choice A is incorrect because human societies do not evolve through the same stages. Each society changes at its own pace and in its own way. Choice C is incorrect because humans have been developing tools for thousands of years prior to the emergence of large urban societies. Choice D is incorrect because people did not need writing to exchange information with one another. Agriculture likely emerged in the prehistoric, not historic, era.

7. **The correct answer is B.** Many archaeologists focus upon prehistoric archaeology (human culture prior to written historical records). Others specialize in historic archaeology, analyzing both the cultural artifacts and written evidence to understand a group of people. Choice A is incorrect because prehistoric and historic archaeologists can conduct research at underwater and terrestrial sites. Choice C is incorrect because historic archaeologists are also interested in artifacts. Choice D is incorrect because paleontologists, not archaeologists, study dinosaurs.

8. **The correct answer is B.** Bronislaw Malinowksi is most famous for his work among the Trobriand Islands communities. Choices A, C, and D are incorrect.

9. **The correct answer is D.** An age group is a group of people of the same age who experience culturally relevant experiences, such as rites of passage, at the same time. Choice A is incorrect because associations based on age do not necessarily mean they have culturally relevant experiences together. Choice B is incorrect because kinship terms are defined as specific ways relatives are labeled or referred to. Choice C is incorrect because an age group means something more than a survey category in anthropology.

10. **The correct answer is D.** Sociolinguists study verbal and non-verbal communication in a variety of social contexts. They use their training to research a particular issue related to human language and develop an appropriate program. Choice A is incorrect because physical anthropologists focus on the biological history and diversity of humanity. Choice B is incorrect because structural linguists examine the construction (the grammar and syntax, for example) of languages. Choice C is incorrect because historic archaeologists analyze both the cultural artifacts and written evidence to understand a group of people.

11. **The correct answer is C.** Mutation refers to random changes in DNA that may lead to beneficial, harmful, or neutral traits for an organism. Choice A is incorrect because genetic drift occurs when random events, such as an earthquake, cause an individual to die without reproducing. Choice B is incorrect because gene flow refers to an individual or individuals from one gene pool introducing genetic material to another gene pool through producing offspring. Choice D is incorrect because phenotype refers to an individual's physical trait or expression of the genotype.

12. **The correct answer is B.** Historic archaeologists analyze both the cultural artifacts and written evidence to understand a group of people. Choices A, C, D are incorrect because those anthropologists are all physical anthropologists. Physical anthropologists focus on the biological history and diversity of humanity. Primatologists conduct biological research and observation of nonhuman primates to shed light on human evolution. Forensic anthropologists use applied biological anthropology to conduct an analysis of skeletal remains.

13. **The correct answer is A.** Bronislaw Malinowksi and others proposed the idea that cultural institutions function to fulfill basic
human biological needs and support the workings of society.
Choice B is incorrect because the Anthropology and Gender
theory focuses on women's roles and how gender is important to
understanding culture. Choice C is incorrect because Postmod-
ernism argues that cultural descriptions are subjective, often
reflect the anthropologist's bias, and can therefore never be accurately or fully described. Choice D is incorrect because the Globalization theory argues that culture must be understood within
the context of the global network connecting capital, resources,
goods, and services.

14. **The correct answer is A.** An ethnocentric perspective refers to
the belief that one's own norms and values are the only correct
standard for living and should be used to judge others. Choice
B is incorrect because the holistic perspective refers to the way
anthropologists understand cultural components by how they
interact with one another. Choice C is incorrect because the
four-field perspective refers to the four subfields of anthropology
(physical, linguistic, archaeology, and cultural) and how they
are used to study humanity. Choice D is incorrect because a
culturally relative perspective argues that each culture must be
understood by its own norms and values and not be immediately
judged by the standards of other cultures.

15. **The correct answer is B.** Scientists refer to all of the possible
genetic variations within the human species as the gene pool.
Choice A is incorrect because a gene pool refers to the entire
species. Choice C is incorrect because the product of a sperm
fertilizing an egg is a zygote (becomes an embryo after implan-
tation). Choice D is incorrect because the gene pool refers to the
genetic differences among humans.

16. **The correct answer is C.** Rites of passage are rituals that mark an individual's movement from one social status or stage of life to another. These include ceremonies for birth, marriage, aging, and death. Choice A is incorrect because witchcraft refers to magical rituals used to cause harm. Choice B is incorrect because rites of intensification (such as going to weekly prayer service) bind a group together and reinforce the norms and values of that group. Choice D is incorrect because rites of purification ritually cleanse a person or group when a taboo has been violated.

17. **The correct answer is D.** From the moment a person is born until the moment he or she passes away, the person is learning to be part of a cultural group, a process called enculturation. Since enculturation is a lifelong process, choices A, B, and C are incorrect.

18. **The correct answer is A.** Every society has rules prohibiting sexual relationships between family members. These incest taboos, however, do not all define family in the same way. Some cultures prohibit relationships between blood relatives. Other cultures encourage marriage between certain cousins but not others. Choice B is incorrect because the four forces of evolution are mutation, genetic drift, gene flow, and natural selection. Choice C is incorrect because the preference for monogamous marriage is not related to the incest taboo. Choice D is incorrect because prohibitions of an incest taboo differ between cultures.

19. **The correct answer is C.** Pastoralists care for and keep herds of domesticated animals such as goats, cattle, or camels. Choice A is incorrect because the long-term breeding of livestock is part of the subsistence strategy of agriculturalists. Choice B is incorrect because pastoralists need large areas for their animals to graze and eat grass. Choice D is incorrect because communal gardens are generally found in horticultural societies.

20. **The correct answer is B.** Shamans are often healers, people who treat and cure medical and spiritual illnesses. Choice A is incorrect because priestesses (and priests) hold a full-time position in the group and are expected to conduct rituals, interact with the supernatural, and lead the community. Choice C is incorrect because some religious groups believe ancestral spirits bind them together as one people and, as a result, have a special relationship with an animal, plant, or other object that represents that spirit (totemism). Choice D is incorrect because, in the religious sense, a pilgrim is someone who travels to a sacred site to prove one's dedication to the faith.

DIAGNOSTIC TEST ASSESSMENT GRID

Now that you've completed the diagnostic test and read through the answer explanations, you can use your results to target your studying. Find the question numbers from the diagnostic test that you answered incorrectly and highlight or circle them below. Then focus extra attention on the sections dealing with those topics.

General Anthropology		
Content Area	**Topic**	**Question #**
Anthropology: Methodologies and Disciplines	• Physical anthropology • Cultural anthropology • Linguistics • Archaeology • Applied anthropology	1, 7
History and Theory	• Ethnographies and perspectives • Sex and gender • Race and ethnicity • Cultural ecology and evolution	8, 13

Physical Anthropology	• Genetic principles
	• Evolutionary principles
	• Primatology
	• Paleontology
	  1. Relative and absolute dating
	  2. Fossil hominids
		2, 11, 15

Archaeology	• Methodology • Paleolithic and Mesolithic • Neolithic • Development of civilization and urban societies	6, 12
Cultural Systems and Processes	• Components of culture • Symbolic systems • Language and communication • Cultural diffusion and power • Cultural universals, sub-cultures and countercultures • World system and colonialism • Arts	3, 14, 17

General Anthropology

Content Area	Topic	Question #
Social Organization	• Marriage and family patterns • Kinship and descent groups • Social and economic stratification	9, 18
Economic and Political Organizations	• Bands, tribes, chiefdoms, and states • Subsistence and settlement patterns • Trade, reciprocity, redistribution, and market exchange • Modern political systems • Globalization and the Environment	4, 19
Religion	• Belief Systems • Formal institutions • Informal organizations • Religious practices and practitioners • Rituals	16, 20

Modernization and Application of Anthropology	• Applied anthropology
	• Cultural preservation
	• Directed and spontaneous cultural change
	• Future directions
	  1. Environment
	  2. Cultural resource management
	  3. Indigenous survival and global culture
		5, 10

Chapter 3

General Anthropology Subject Review

ANTHROPOLOGY: METHODOLOGIES AND DISCIPLINES

From the Greek *anthropos* ("human") and *logia* ("study"), anthropology is the study of humankind from our earliest hominid ancestors to current cultures and societies. The discipline covers the whole of human existence, as seen through its four major subdisciplines: physical, cultural, linguistic, and archaeology.

Physical Anthropology

Physical anthropology focuses on the biological history and diversity of humanity. Physical anthropologists (also known as biological anthropologists) study human evolution: adaptation to the environment over the millennia. Researchers in this subdiscipline might further specialize in one of several branches. We'll review the following three in this chapter:

1. *Human variation*: study of biological differences (physiology, genetics, etc.) within the human species
2. *Primatology*: biological research and observation of nonhuman primates to shed light on human evolution
3. *Paleoanthropology*: reconstruction of humanity's evolutionary past using the fossil record

Later on, we will explore important terms and concepts (such as fossil hominids, genetics, and living primates) associated with physical anthropology and these specializations.

Cultural Anthropology

Cultural anthropology focuses on researching and comparing patterns of human cultural diversity. An **ethnographer** spends an extended period of time with a group of people observing, interviewing, and participating in the activities of their everyday lives. Based on the data collected, the ethnographer will often produce a written account (called an **ethnography**) of that time period with detailed descriptions of the shared behavioral patterns, values, and norms of that group. The practice of comparing and contrasting the cultural patterns of one group with other ethnographic examples is referred to as **ethnology**. Later in this chapter we will discuss some of the different structures found in cultural groups such as religion, kinship, and economic and political organizations.

Linguistic Anthropology

Linguistic anthropology is the study of human language. Three specific branches within this subdiscipline examine the complex variations in human communication:

1. *Historical linguistics* is concerned with the connection between languages and how these languages change over time.
2. *Descriptive or structural linguistics* examines the construction (the grammar and syntax, for example) of languages.
3. *Sociolinguistics* studies verbal and nonverbal communication in a variety of social contexts.

We will review linguistic anthropology in relationship to the concept of culture and highlight important terms and definitions (see Cultural Systems and Processes).

Archaeology

Archaeology is the study of prehistoric and historic human cultures based on their material remains. Through the excavation of sites with evidence of human activity, archaeologists carefully recover, catalog, and study items created and/or shaped by people (artifacts). These sites, which may be terrestrial (on land) or aquatic (underwater), can yield information that predates written history. Therefore, many archaeologists focus on prehistoric archaeology (human culture prior to written historical records). Others specialize in historic archaeology, analyzing both the cultural artifacts and written evidence to understand a group of people.

We will review these topics in greater detail, including the differences between the Paleolithic, Mesolithic, and Neolithic eras and the rise of civilization and urban societies.

Applied Anthropology

While anthropology is typically divided into the four subfields, anthropologists are debating the inclusion of a fifth subdiscipline: **applied anthropology**. As the name suggests, this subdiscipline uses the perspective and tools of physical, archaeological, linguistic, and cultural anthropology to solve a variety of problems. At the end of this chapter, we will go over examples of applied anthropology and highlight situations where an anthropological perspective might be the most useful.

Regardless of the number of subdisciplines and specializations, one of the unifying principles of anthropology is the **holistic perspective**. The holistic perspective explains, in part, the four-field approach in anthropology. Anthropologists strive to understand the totality of human existence and believe that in order to do so, we must examine how all of the different components (cultural, biological, material, etc.) interact with one another. We will revisit this idea throughout the chapter.

HISTORY AND THEORY

Ethnographies and Perspectives

The early history of anthropology was characterized by what some call "armchair anthropology." Instead of participant observation, scholars of the late nineteenth century would read accounts about other cultures (from explorers, missionaries, reporters, historians, etc.) and draw conclusions based on that information. Lewis Henry Morgan and Edward Burnett Tylor were among the most famous of these anthropologists who worked out of an office or study and made sweeping generalizations about a world they never experienced. Morgan and Tylor were the chief authors, for example, of the theory of **cultural evolution**. Based on their readings, they argued that every cultural group in the world should evolve through three stages: savagery, barbarism, and civilization. Morgan's and Tylor's ethnocentric perspective was that their own Western society was the most evolved and therefore the highest standard everyone should aspire to.

Franz Boas was a United States-based anthropologist and fierce critic of cultural evolution. He lived and conducted research among the North American Inuit on Baffin Island. Boas's subsequent research among other indigenous groups convinced him that cultures should be understood by their own internal norms and values. Cultural evolutionism, he argued, was constructed of racist categories based on misinformation and little to no understanding of the realities of the world's cultural diversity. Boas's research philosophy and the work of his students (who would later become his peers) influenced the discipline's rejection of ethnocentrism and cultural evolution. They focused on cultural relativism and **cultural determinism** (how culture shapes an individual's personality).

Boas was an example of an **ethnographer**: a cultural anthropologist who spends an extended period of time with a group of people observing, interviewing, and participating in the activities of their everyday lives. This activity is referred to as **participant observation**. Anthropologists focus on understanding the **emic** perspective: the point of view of the person who is part of that cultural group.

Based on the data collected, the anthropologist will often produce a written account (called an **ethnography**) of that time period with detailed descriptions of that culture. The analysis of those cultural patterns is usually written from the **etic** perspective: the point of view of someone who is outside of that cultural group. The practice of comparing and contrasting the cultural patterns of one group with other ethnographic examples is referred to as **ethnology**.

Polish-born anthropologist Bronislaw Malinowski pioneered the core anthropological method of participant observation. He spent several years (1915–1918) among the people of the Trobriand Islands and concluded that cultural groups must be understood by their own internal logics—not by the logics of others.

Since the time of Boas and Malinowski, anthropologists have continued researching cultural groups, introducing different methods and debating about the relationship between people and culture.

Cultural ecology, for example, focuses specifically on how the physical environment is the main reason for culture change. Over time, these debates and discussions have been categorized by how they help anthropologists explain and interpret culture.

The following chart briefly summarizes some of these anthropological theories.

Theory	Explanations and Interpretations of Culture	Key Contributors
Cultural Evolution	Cultural development evolves through universal stages.	Lewis Henry Morgan Edward Tylor
Historical Particularism	Cultures must be understood through the history that produced them.	Franz Boas Alfred Kroeber Benjamin Whorf
Functionalism	Cultural institutions function to fulfill basic human biological needs and support the workings of society.	Bronislaw Malinowski A.R. Radcliffe-Brown
Culture and Personality	Culture shapes and is shaped by the personalities of each individual.	Ruth Benedict Margaret Mead
Cultural Ecology and Neo-evolutionary Thought	Culture adapts to the physical environment.	Julian Steward Leslie White
Ecological Materialism	Environment and people influence culture and vice versa.	Morton Fried Marvin Harris
Structuralism	A universal human culture is the product of the human brain.	Claude Lévi-Strauss
Ethnoscience and Cognitive Anthropology	Culture reveals how people categorize the world, which, in turn, reveals how the human mind functions.	Harold Conklin Stephen Tyler
Sociobiology	Culture is a product of human genetics.	E.O.Wilson
Anthropology and Gender	Women's roles and how gender is construed is important to understanding culture.	Sherry Ortner Sally Slocum
Symbolic and Interpretive Anthropology	Understanding a culture means studying the significance of the symbols it uses.	Mary Douglas Clifford Geertz Victor Turner

Theory	Explanations and Interpretations of Culture	Key Contributors
Postmodernism	Cultural descriptions are subjective, often reflect the anthropologist's bias, and can therefore never be accurately or fully described.	Renato Rosaldo Vincent Crapanzano
Globalization	Culture must be understood within the context of the global network connecting capital, resources, goods, and services.	Arjun Appadurai James Ferguson Akhil Gupta

Sex and Gender

In anthropology, the terms **sex** and **gender** are defined differently. **Gender** commonly refers to the cultural norms, values, expectations, and categories of what is "masculine" and "feminine." In the past century of anthropological study, the meaning of the word *gender* has shifted and now encompasses perspectives that no longer conform to long-held beliefs and assumptions about the roles of men and women in society. For example, the Hijras of India are neither gender male or female and are referred to as "third gender." Other cultures have fourth or fifth genders. Gender male or female does not always correspond to sex male or sex female. People may be identified as belonging to a specific gender (at birth, for example) and people may self-identify as belonging to a particular gender (the Hijras of India, for example).

Race and Ethnicity

Race refers to certain physical traits grouped together under specific labels and categories. As discussed above, human variations in skin tone, eye and hair color, height, etc., are due to evolution and other environmental factors. Genetic testing identifies each of us as belonging to a single human species. However, over time and often in relation to systems of stratification, the idea that humans were separate "races" became accepted as natural and correct. Human beings owning other human beings who are stripped of their rights and freedoms (**slavery**) occurred in many cultures over the centuries. However, slavery from the fifteenth through nineteenth centuries was justified, in part, by the idea that indigenous African peoples were of a different, lower "race" than Europeans. Although "race" does not exist biologically, it is still used to justify social stratification.

Ethnicity refers to being part of a select social group with a common cultural tradition and/or national origin. While race is based primarily on physical traits, ethnicity is often categorized in terms of one's common ancestry, a shared history, language, and regional culture.

To illustrate the difference between race and ethnicity, consider two people—one from the United States and one from Sweden. Based on their physical characteristics—light skin and eyes, thin lips, narrow noses, and straight hair—both would be considered members of the Caucasian race. However, their ethnicities could be quite different—they most likely would speak different languages, have different traditions, and perhaps different beliefs as a result of the environments in which they were raised.

PHYSICAL ANTHROPOLOGY

Physical (or biological) anthropologists focus on the biological history and diversity of humanity. Some choose specialization in different areas and focus on particular questions. Physical anthropologists interested in **human variation** ask, "What is the range of biological diversity within the human species, and how does it happen?" **Primatologists** research answers to the question, "What can biological study and observation of nonhuman primates tell us about human evolution?" A **paleoanthropologist** asks, "What does the fossil record tell us about the ancestors and relatives of *Homo sapiens*?"

Answers to these questions are rooted in Charles Darwin's Theory of Evolution. In the 1830s, Darwin was part of a scientific expedition that exposed him to animal and plant life in various coastal areas around the world. Based on his observations and extensive background knowledge of science and history, Darwin eventually proposed his now-famous theory of evolution by natural selection. Simply, Darwin argued that every species of plant and animal life exhibits a range of variation. These variations may help an organism survive or die in its environment. If a variation (also referred to as a **trait**) is considered advantageous, the organism possessing it will survive to reproduce and pass those traits to offspring. If the variation is considered disadvantageous, the organism dies and will not reproduce. Generation after generation, only those organisms with traits that help them survive the environment will live to reproduce and, eventually, new species will emerge.

However, Darwin did not have the answers to questions of how exactly these traits were passed on to offspring and why the variations occurred. Unbeknownst to Darwin, in 1866, a monk named Gregor Mendel published some of the information crucial to answering these questions. Mendel was a scientist who used the monastery garden to grow and study approximately 30,000 pea plants over ten years. He identified specific traits of the plants (flower color, height, etc.) and recorded how these traits were (or were not) passed along from one generation to the next. Based on these data, Mendel eventually identified specific patterns that are now referred to as **Mendel's Principles of Inheritance**, which we will discuss in more detail shortly.

> **TIP:** Each human cell contains 23 pairs of chromosomes, for a total of 46 per cell.

Genetic Principles

Over the years, scientists have built on Darwin's and Mendel's work to give us a clearer understanding of what happens at the cellular and genetic level. You may remember from your life science classes that all animal and plant life is composed of cells. Under the power of a microscope, you can see chromosomes located in the cell nucleus.

These chromosomes are comprised of DNA (deoxyribonucleic acid) strands. **Genes**, which are also referred to as the units of heredity, are specific sections of DNA. In the human body, genes are the genetic blueprints for making proteins. These proteins drive the development and maintenance of the human body and are what cause people to have different traits such as eye or hair color and blood type.

Scientists have identified genes that may cause more than one version of a particular trait. For example, Mendel observed that pea plants grew to different heights. Scientists today could say that the gene for the height trait comes in a "tall gene" or "short gene" variety. To help clarify between these different terms, scientists today use the term **allele**. The height trait genes will cause a pea plant to be a different size because of presence of the "tall" trait allele or the "short" trait allele.

Mendel's Principles of Inheritance outline how these traits are inherited by offspring.

- **The principle of segregation** states that each organism usually has two alleles of each gene. When a sperm fertilizes an egg and the cell begins to reproduce, the offspring will receive one allele of each gene from each parent.
- **The principle of dominance** states one allele will dominate over the other. **Dominant alleles** will produce dominant traits. **Recessive alleles** will produce a trait only if a dominant allele is not present.
- **The principle of independent assortment** states that the genes for different traits are inherited independently of one another.

In humans, genes are responsible for the production of blood. Blood type is a trait that actually has three alleles: A, B, and O. Offspring will inherit one blood allele from each parent (**the principle of segregation**). Scientists have determined that the A allele is dominant to the O allele; the B allele is also dominant to the O allele (**the principle of dominance**). The A allele and B allele are actually co-dominant, which means that both traits of the allele will be expressed. Therefore, depending upon which allele is inherited from the parent, the offspring will have a blood type of A, B, AB, or O. Finally, the blood trait and hair trait (for example) are inherited independently of one another (**the principle of independent assortment**).

		Father's Blood Type				
		A	B	AB	O	
Mother's Blood Type	A	A or O	A, B, AB, or O	A, B, or AB	A or O	Child's Blood Type
	B	A, B, AB, or O	B or O	A, B, or AB	B or O	
	AB	A, B, or AB	A, B, or AB	A, B, or AB	A or B	
	O	A or O	B or O	A or B	O	

In addition to blood type, the diversity of physical traits among humans suggests a variety of possible allele combinations. A **genotype** refers to the genes and alleles each person possesses. The **phenotype** refers to the physical expression of the genotype. A person may have inherited alleles for dark (for example, black) and light (for example, blond) hair from their parents. However, because dark hair is a dominant allele trait and light hair is a recessive allele trait, a dark hair color will grow from the person's head. The dark hair allele expresses itself on the human body.

Evolutionary Principles

Within the human species, all of these possible genetic variations are referred to as the **gene pool**. Returning to Darwin, how do scientists know if humans are evolving? The answer lies in how the frequency of alleles in the gene pool changes over time. The percentages of allele expression among the human population change over the years and centuries. Scientists have summarized the reasons why as **the four forces of evolution**:

1. *Mutation* refers to random changes in DNA that may lead to beneficial, harmful, or neutral traits for an organism.
2. *Genetic drift* occurs in smaller populations when random events such as an earthquake cause an individual to die without reproducing. That individual's genotype disappears from the gene pool, which decreases the number of available alleles to be passed on to the next generation.
3. *Gene flow* occurs when an individual or individuals from one gene pool introduces genetic material to another gene pool through producing offspring.
4. *Natural selection* is the process through which individuals who have traits that allow them to survive in their environment and reproduce pass along these traits to their offspring, thereby increasing the frequency of those alleles in the gene pool. The alleles of those who do not reproduce are lost, thereby reducing the frequency of those alleles in the gene pool.

Physical anthropologists ask, "What is the range of biological diversity within the human species and how does it happen?" The human gene pool is filled with a variety of alleles (genotypes) that may or may not express themselves physically (phenotypes). Adaptation to Earth's environment has produced humans with a broad range of body shapes, for example. Differences in other phenotypes, such as skin tone and eye and face shape, also have genetic explanations.

···

TIP: A monkey will make a distinct sound to warn other monkeys of predators. Primatologists try teaching gorillas sign language.

···

Primatology

Primatologists ask, "What can biological study and observation of nonhuman primates tell us about human evolution?" By learning how **living primates** such as gorillas and chimpanzees have adapted over time (evolution by natural selection), primatologists help us understand how humans may have changed over the millennia.

In the research field (forest, jungles, etc.), primatologists spend years observing various primate groups. The results of the anthropologists' studies have yielded a wide variety of insights as to how they live and survive in the wild.

- Orangutans (found in Sumatra and Borneo) are generally solitary creatures that tend to forage for food over broad areas. Female orangutans stay with their offspring until they have matured to self-sufficiency. These primates have been observed attempting to spear fish and catch termites with branches.
- Gorillas in sub-Saharan Africa eat plants, fruits, and insects. They live in groups: usually one older, dominant male with younger males, females, and offspring. Gorillas have been observed building nests of branches and leaves.
- Chimpanzees are found in East, Central, and West Africa and live in large groups of approximately sixty individuals. While they mostly eat fruit, like other primates they also eat insects and plants. Chimpanzees have also been seen eating meat. Primatologists have observed chimpanzees using sticks to pull termites out of a nest and rocks to break open nuts.

In a laboratory setting, primatologists study every aspect of these nonhuman primates. The same advances that allow research at the human genetic level have been used to discover that chimpanzees (for example) share 98 percent of the same DNA with humans. DNA also reveals how primates are related to one another. Primatologists study feces, hair, and teeth for clues about diet. The different skeletal structures of the primates are studied to determine why they move the way they do.

Primatologists contribute to the broader understanding of humans by studying our closest primate relatives. How have primates evolved in response to environmental pressures? How do they survive in the wild? How do they learn? How do they communicate with one another? Anthropologists compare the answers to these, and other questions, with similar research conducted with humans. Comparisons help us understand how much behavior is driven by nature (biology) and how much is driven by nurture (teaching, learning).

Paleontology/Paleoanthropology

A **paleoanthropologist** asks, "What does the fossil record tell us about the ancestors and relatives of *Homo sapiens*?" **Fossil** refers to the preserved remains of an organism (plant, animal, human) found in the Earth's crust (or glaciers, marshes, etc.). When a paleoanthropologist discovers a fossil, he or she attempts to find out how old it is through relative and absolute dating.

- **Relative dating** methods can tell us only if a fossil is older or younger than another fossil. Stratigraphy is one example of a relative dating method. Generally, deeper layers of dirt and rock are older than the surface layer of dirt. Through a variety of other techniques, scientists have determined how old these layers are going back millions of years. Paleontologists can determine the age of a fossil based on how far below the ground's surface it is found; simply, the fossil's age is relative to the age of the earth around it.

- **Absolute dating** (also known as **calendar dating**) tells the age of something in actual years. For example, if human remains are found next to a coin with the year 1500 inscribed on it, scientists can tell that the remains date back to sometime during or after the year 1500. Another form of absolute dating is called carbon-14 (C-14) dating. Living organisms have the same amount of carbon-14 in their cellular structure. Once an organism dies, C-14 begins decreasing at a constant rate. Scientists test fossils for the amount of C-14 present, and, with that number, they can tell how long ago an organism lived.

The improvement of dating techniques has helped paleoanthropologists identify the biological origins of modern humans (*Homo sapiens*). Based on what we know about evolution, anthropologists generally accept that many species came before *Homo sapiens*. Over millions of years, their bodies adapted and changed in response to the environment. Those who had traits best suited for survival passed along those characteristics to offspring. Paleoanthropologists have grouped together fossils they believe represent specific groups of humanity's ancestors.

The following chart presents some of those groups.

Name	Approximate Dates Alive	Fossil Discovered at Sites in These Countries (partial list)	Distinguishing Physical Traits and Behaviors (partial list)	Cultural Characteristics (partial list)
Australopithecus afarenis	4–2.9 million years ago	• Ethiopia • Tanzania	• Ape-like features • Walked upright on two legs (also known as bipedal)	• *Australopithecus afarenis* likely used tools like modern chimpanzees.
Homo habilis	2.8–1.5 million years ago	• Kenya • Tanzania	• Smaller teeth than *Australopithecus* • Larger brain than *Australopithecus*	• Oldowan stone tools are rocks shaped by striking flakes off. Both the core rock and flakes were used for cutting or slicing plants and animals.
Homo erectus	1.8 million to 300,000 years ago	• China • Indonesia • Kenya	• Large molars • More robust than average modern humans	• Acheulan stone tools are oval-shaped hand axes produced like Oldowan tools. • Some evidence suggests that the controlled use of fire dates from this time period.
Homo neanderthalensis	250,000 to 30,000 years ago	• Belgium • France • Iraq	• Shorter and stockier than modern humans • Powerful muscles • Thicker and heavier skeletal structure than modern humans	• Mousterian stone tools refer to the variety of objects, such as hand axes and wooden spears, found at various sites. • Anthropologists have discovered caves with fossils, which suggest *Homo neanderthalensis* deliberately buried their dead. Master the
Homo sapiens	100,000 years ago to present	• Israel • South Africa	• Large brains • Smaller teeth	• Cave art discovered in France dates to over 30,000 years ago; tools date to over 40,000 years ago.

Advances in genetic testing and the discovery of other fossils have helped fill in some of the gaps in our understanding of human evolution. Anthropologists believe, for example, that humans evolved on the African continent and eventually migrated around the world. DNA testing suggests that *Homo sapiens* and *Homo neanderthalensis* likely interbred. New discoveries suggest other species existed that may or may not have been ancestors to humans.

Biological anthropology is the subfield that focuses on the biological history and diversity of humanity. In comparing human variation past and present, studying genetic relatives of *Homo sapiens*, and understanding the biological processes at work, anthropologists understand humanity down to its DNA. This is, however, only one piece of the human puzzle that must be understood in context with archaeology, linguistics, and cultural anthropology (**holism**).

ARCHAEOLOGY

Methodology

Archaeology is the study of prehistoric and historic human cultures based on their material remains. Archaeologists share similar methods with paleoanthropologists: both carefully excavate sites and use absolute and relative dating to help determine the age of fossils or artifacts (items created and/ or shaped by people). These anthropologists carefully recover, catalog, and study their findings to give us a more compete history of humanity.

Archaeologists study sites with evidence of human activity; these sites may be terrestrial (on land) or underwater. Maritime archaeologists search for shipwrecks in oceans or lakes, for example, or search for evidence of coastal human settlements that have been submerged over time. Artifacts can yield information that predates written history. Therefore, many archaeologists focus upon **prehistoric archaeology** (human culture prior to written historical records). Others specialize in **historic archaeology**, analyzing both the cultural artifacts and written evidence to understand a group of people.

Paleolithic, Mesolithic, and Neolithic Eras

Archaeologists categorize the human past based on the type of tools used by our ancestors. These dates are approximate and subject to change based on new discoveries by anthropologists. Overlap between the dates is possible because changes in tool use happened gradually over time in different places.

Paleolithic (Old Stone Age)

- **Lower Paleolithic:** 2.8 million to 1.5 million years ago: *Homo habilis* used Oldowan stone tools, which refer to rocks that were shaped by striking flakes off with other rocks. Both the core rock and flakes were used for cutting or slicing plants and animals.
- **Middle Paleolithic:** 250,000 to 30,000 years ago: *Homo neanderthalensis* used Mousterian stone tools, which refer to the variety of objects, such as hand axes and wooden spears, found at various sites.
- **Upper Paleolithic:** 40,000 to 10,000 years ago: Cave art likely produced by *Homo sapiens* discovered in France dates to over 30,000 years ago. Tools found at other sites date to over 40,000 years ago.

Mesolithic (Middle Stone Age) refers to the transition era between the Paleolithic and the Neolithic. Humans inhabit every continent on Earth.

Neolithic (New Stone Age)

- **Early Neolithic:** 12,000 to 10,000 years ago: *Homo sapiens* manufactured, among other things, arrowheads and blades. Humans began engaging in food production, also known as **agriculture**.
- **Late Neolithic:** 10,000 to 5,000 years ago: *Homo sapiens* manufactured, among other things, pottery. The emergence of writing and record keeping mark the end of the prehistoric era.

During the Paleolithic era, humans survived by **foraging**: collecting plants, fishing, and hunting animals in order to survive. Humans probably lived in small groups, moving from place to place as the seasons changed, vegetation died and grew, and animals moved. The Neolithic era marks a profound shift in how humans survived. Archaeological evidence suggests that **agriculture**, the deliberate production of food by growing crops and tending animals, slowly emerged in many (but not all) cultures around the world. Depending on the environmental factors (temperature, soil, etc.), availability of plants, variety of animals to domesticate, and availability of materials to make tools with means this **Neolithic Revolution** did not happen abruptly. Each cultural group learned agricultural techniques at its own pace, although most of these changes occurred 12,000 to 10,000 years ago.

TIP: The soil around some remains of *Homo neanderthalensis* and Mousterian tool sets have revealed ancient traces of pollen, which helps anthropologists reconstruct which plants were possibly important to Neanderthals.

Development of Civilization and Urban Societies

The transition from foraging to agriculture meant that people could stay in one place rather than move on a regular basis. Humans began guiding the growth of plants and the reproduction of animals (also referred to as **domestication**). People had a relatively consistent source of food. Increased food production and population growth transformed small villages into larger towns. As technology improved, agriculture became even more productive. Farmland could now support larger city centers.

Governments emerged to manage the needs of the large populace. Social hierarchies meant people began experiencing unequal access to important resources (**social stratification**). Archaeology is the subfield of anthropology that focuses on the study of material remains. From tools found with our earliest ancestors to vases in the hull of a ship on the ocean floor, artifacts tell stories of the human experience. However, the interpretation of these artifacts happens within a larger context. While **processual** archaeologists believe they can come to an objective conclusion about the significance of an artifact, **post-processual** archaeologists argue that all interpretation is subject to bias. Is an artifact significant? What is the meaning of this artifact to the people who produced it? Is this artifact representative of one cultural group or another?

To avoid interpretations that only reflect the archaeologist's viewpoint, post-processual archaeologists say the answers to these and other questions should be supported (when possible) with other evidence. This is another interpretation of the anthropological focus on the holistic perspective. In archaeology, the artifacts should be understood in relationship to other available information. In prehistoric archaeology, this might mean biological and chemical analysis of the soil around the artifact. In historic anthropology, written records can be consulted to help reconstruct the significance of artifacts.

Broadly, archaeologists' research also adds another piece to the human puzzle: physical anthropologists help us understand our human biology. Archaeology helps us understand how we physically interact with the world around us.

Linguistic and cultural anthropology add to the physical pieces we've already covered to help us understand the rest of the human experience.

CULTURAL SYSTEMS AND PROCESSES

Components of Culture

Another perspective that helps unify the four fields of anthropological research is the concept of **culture**. Physical anthropologists explore human biology and its relationship to culture. Archaeologists study artifacts and the culture. Linguistic anthropologists research our human capacity for language and how it is directly related to culture. Cultural anthropology focuses on researching and comparing patterns and components of human cultural diversity. What is culture?

Culture Is Learned

Unlike the physical traits we discussed in the section on genetic principles, culture is *not* passed along to the next generation through our DNA. From the moment we are born until the moment we pass away, we are learning to be part of a cultural group, a process called **enculturation**. Like nonhuman primates, we learn through observation of the world around us. However, we also learn the culturally appropriate behavioral patterns, values, and norms from other people (caregivers, peers, professors, etc.). Communication through language, gestures, pictures, and written records helps us learn the information and skills we need to survive in our environment.

Culture Is Shared

Cultural groups define their **norms** (the way things should be done) and **values** (standards for what is good, correct, ethical, and moral). Being a part of that cultural group generally means a shared acceptance of those norms and values. However, anthropologists have observed a difference between **real** and **ideal culture**. A group may state certain norms and values (**ideal culture**) but those norms and values are not necessarily acted out in reality (**real culture**). For example, a cultural group may say that an ideal marriage is monogamous and based in romantic love. However, the reality may be that people marry for any number of reasons, including financial gain or family pressure.

Culture Is a System of Symbols

As we discussed earlier, symbols represent something else. In human language, words (spoken and written) are symbols because they represent ideas, actions, objects, people, animals, plants, etc. Objects—such as flags for example—can also be symbols if they are significant to a cultural group. All of these symbols help people organize and understand the world around them. We have words and names for the things around us. We can communicate about what we see, hear, touch, and imagine. We can transmit information about our norms and values through the objects we create or shape (our material culture or, from an archaeological perspective, artifacts).

Culture Is an Integrated System

Anthropologists recognize many different aspects of culture, including economic systems, political organization, religion, kinship, and others we will review later. These systems interact with one another; in order to understand a culture, they must be understood in relationship to one another. Anthropologists study how well (or poorly) these pieces are integrated and function together.

Culture Is Adaptive

As you may recall from our earlier discussion about biological anthropology, humans evolve biologically in response to changing environments. Human culture also changes and adapts to give people a better chance to survive and reproduce in their environment. For example, in the space of a few years, a cultural group who is used to hunting game and gathering food in a forest might find its territory destroyed due to natural disaster like a drought. In order to survive, the group will develop new cultural practices to find and process food from other sources.

Culture Is Constantly Changing

Cultural change happens quickly or slowly, and cultures change at different speeds from one another. There is no blueprint or chart for when and how a cultural group might experience any change. Why do cultures change? Environmental pressures, disease, natural disasters are some reasons; conflict within the group or from outside of the group is another reason. Cultures may also change due to **invention** (the development or discovery of something completely new) or **innovation** (the improvement or change to something that already exists). **Diffusion** is also responsible for culture change: ideas, devices, and/or innovations that spread from one culture to another.

Debates About Culture

Cultural universals refer to something that is present in all cultures. Anthropologists debate about what counts as a universal and if they do, in fact, exist in all cultures. Biologically, for example, all humans need to eat, drink, and sleep. However, different norms exist about what is considered "food" and where someone should sleep. Cultural anthropologists have observed patterns of human behavior that seem to exist in multiple, but certainly not all, cultures.

Similarly, some anthropologists continue debating the components of culture. Can culture be compartmentalized? Early anthropologist Edward Tylor first proposed a definition of culture: "Culture... taken in its broad, ethnographic sense, is that complex whole which includes knowledge, belief, art, morals, law, custom, and any other capabilities and habits acquired by man as a member of society." Since then, some anthropologists suggest the basic components of culture are its symbols, language, norms and values. Other argue that beliefs or technology (and other categories) belong on the list.

Culture shapes who we are, what we think, and what we do. Anthropologists argue over **agency**: people's ability to make choices and exercise their free will. Are we ever truly free to behave outside cultural norms, and values? What happens when an individual identifies as part of a culture but rejects some of those norms and values? Is it possible to measure how much of an individual's decision making is rooted in enculturation or his or her own free will?

Studying Culture

A cultural anthropologist may decide to focus on a specific **culture**: a group that shares behavioral patterns, values, and norms. Anthropologists ask questions about **society**, a group of people who usually (but not always) share the same culture, live in a specific territory, and share common goals.

Most cultural anthropologists, like post-processual archaeologists, are particularly aware of their own biases. Anthropologists argue against **ethnocentrism**, the belief that one's own norms and values are the only correct standard for living and should be used to judge others. Anthropologists begin with a method referred to as **cultural relativism**, which argues that each culture must be understood by its own norms and values and not be immediately judged by the standards of other cultures.

Art, for example, is often subject to fierce debates. **Art** is broadly defined as expression of the human imagination and includes, but is not limited to, music, song, dance, drawing, carving, paintings, poems, and stories. What fits into the categories of art and how it is valued depends on each cultural group.

Symbols, Language, and Communication

Linguistic anthropology is the study of human language: a system of communication that includes symbols, sounds, and gestures. A **symbol** is something that represents something else. In human language, spoken and written words are symbols because they represent ideas, actions, objects, people, animals, plants, etc. In the English language, for example, individual letters combine to form the word *rose*, which represents a specific type of flower. Humans also combine sounds to produce words, which we can use to communicate with others. Finally, body movements (hand gestures, facial expression, etc.) also communicate specific moods, ideas, and emotions.

Language allows humans to communicate complex ideas, accumulate information (through writing or oral history, for example), and discuss events that occurred in the past, are happening in the present, or could happen in the future. Scientists suggest that animals are able to communicate with one another and, to a certain extent, with humans. However, the evidence suggests that humans' capacity for language and what it helps us accomplish is unmatched by any other species.

Three specific branches within this subdiscipline examine the complex variations in human communication:

1. *Descriptive or structural linguistics* examines the construction of languages. **Phonology** studies the sounds of language and **morphology** examines how words are created from those sounds. Structural linguists also study the **grammar** (the rules of how a language is written and/or spoken) as well as **syntax** (the rules for constructing sentences). A structural linguist might go to a cultural group with no tradition of written history and try to record (through writing as well as video and audio) their language.

2. *Historical linguistics* is concerned with the connection between languages and how these languages change over time. A historical linguist might be interested in how Spanish, Italian, and French, for example, developed from Latin over hundreds of years.

3. *Sociolinguistics* studies verbal and nonverbal communication in a variety of social contexts. These anthropologists are interested in the relationship between culture (discussed extensively below) and language. Specifically, sociolinguists research how age, class, race, ethnicity, gender, and other aspects of a person's background and identity influence communication. For example, how do students communicate with peers compared with speaking to teachers?

SOCIAL ORGANIZATION

A society may be understood by its subsistence strategy, economic system, political organization, and social organization. Anthropologists distinguish between societies where individuals and groups may have different access to goods and services, wealth, status, and power. Anthropologists also study how societies organize themselves at the level of family and kin.

Marriage and Family Patterns

Marriage is a cultural institution that defines the parameters of a union between two or more people, establishes rules for the responsibility of children, and clarifies the relationship between the kin of the married people. The rules regarding **divorce** (the end of a marriage) are also culturally determined.

Every society has rules prohibiting sexual relationships between family members. These **incest taboos**, however, do not all define family in the same way. Some cultures prohibit relationships between blood relatives. Other cultures encourage marriage between certain cousins, but not others.

Other culturally based rules require people marry within their own group (**endogamy**) or outside their own group (**exogamy**). These groups may include class, caste, religious, ethnic, racial, etc. Even the number of spouses one has can differ from group to group. **Monogamy** (only one spouse at a time) is the norm for many cultures but **polygamy** (multiple spouse marriage) also exists. **Polygyny** (the marriage of one man to several women) is sanctioned by some religious groups. **Polyandry** (the marriage of one woman to several men) has been observed in places like Tibet where brothers may marry one woman to keep land intact and within the family (rather than splitting the inheritance between several monogamous married couples).

Finding a spouse or spouses may be left up to the individual. However, anthropologists have also studied **arranged marriage**, where the families of potential spouses determine if their children would be a socially appropriate match.

After marriage, cultural rules determine where the spouses will live:

- **Neolocal:** spouses live separately from their parents in their own households
- **Bilocal** or **ambilocal:** spouses choose which family to live with or near
- **Matrilocal:** spouses live with or near the wife's family
- **Patrilocal:** spouses live with or near the husband's family
- **Avunculocal:** spouses live with or near the husband's mother's brother

Culture defines both marriage and **family.** A **nuclear family** (also known as a **conjugal family**) refers to the married partners and the children they are responsible for. **Extended family** refers to multiple generations of family members: grandparents, married offspring, and grandchildren. From the perspective of the individual, the **natal family** is the group they are born into. How that group is defined depends on the rules of kinship and **descent**.

Kinship and Descent Groups

Descent is how a culture defines how individuals are related to their parents. In **bilateral descent**, descent is traced through both the paternal (father's) and maternal (mother's) line. An individual's **kindred** refers to their maternal and paternal blood relatives.

In **unilateral** (also known as unilineal) **descent**, descent is traced through either the **patrilineal** (male) or **matrilineal** (female) line. A **lineage** is a unilineal kinship group descended from a common ancestor. **Matrilineages** trace descent through the female line; **patrilineages** trace descent through the male line. A **clan** is often composed of many lineages who believe they are descended from a common ancestor many generations before. A **phratry** is at least two clans who believe they are related to one another. When a society is divided into two major descent groups, each half is referred to as a **moiety**. Each moiety usually consists of several clans.

Kinship refers to a network of relatives related by blood or marriage. **Kinship systems** are the ways in which a cultural group classify how people are related to one another. **Kinship terminology** refers to specific ways relatives are labeled. Three popular systems are named for the ethnographic example anthropologists use to describe each system.

The Eskimo system focuses on the nuclear family. Relatives share common labels, such as *aunt*, *uncle*, and *cousin*.

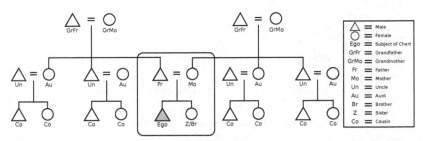

In the Hawaiian system, all of the relatives of the same generation and sex share the same label. An individual's mother, mother's sister, and father's sister share a single term (for example, *mother*). An individual's father, father's brother, and mother's brother share a single term (for example, *father*). An individual's cousins in the same generation are all brothers or sisters.

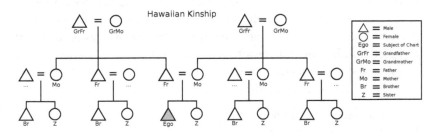

In the Iroquois system, an individual's father and father's brother share a single term (for example, *father*) and a mother and mother's sister share a single term (for example, *mother*). The children of the mother's sister or father's brother are **parallel cousins** to the individual and referred to as *brother* or *sister*.

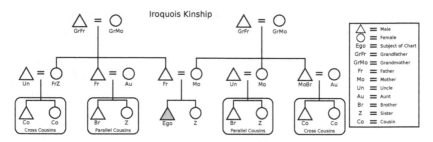

A father's sister may be referred to as an "aunt" and mother's brother may be referred to as an "uncle." The children of the mother's brother or the father's sister are **cross-cousins** to the individual.

SOCIAL AND ECONOMIC STRATIFICATION

In **egalitarian** societies, people generally have about the same access to goods and services, wealth, status, and power. Foraging societies tend to be egalitarian. In **rank** societies, chiefs or other people may have a higher status than others in the group, but everyone still has the same access to goods and services, wealth, status, and power. In **stratified** societies, social and economic hierarchies are normal and the different levels have unequal access to goods and services, wealth, status, and power. These hierarchies are referred to as **social stratification**.

State societies with large populations and economic specialization tend to be stratified societies. **Open class** refers to stratified systems where there is a possibility of moving between the different levels of a social hierarchy. In the open class system, where a person is located in the hierarchy is based on **achieved status**: what a person is able accomplish through their own actions. In the United States, the class system is theoretically open. The "American Dream" says that if people work hard enough, they can earn more money and access to material resources and become part of the upper class (the highest level of the social and economic hierarchy).

Closed class refers to stratified systems where there is no possibility of moving between the different levels of a social hierarchy. In the closed class system, a person's location in the hierarchy is based on **ascribed status**: the position a person was born into. In a **caste** system, one example of a closed class stratified system, a person's position is fixed for life and cannot be changed. Traditionally, the Hindu caste system of India strictly associates people born into it with specific occupations, dress, rituals, and customs.

ECONOMIC AND POLITICAL ORGANIZATION

Economics studies human decision-making regarding the finite amount of goods and services around us. Time, land, meat, vegetables, wood, water, minerals, etc., are in limited supply, and economists study how people choose to use, create, distribute, and work with these resources. Some anthropological debates about the relationship between economics and culture draw from economic theory. The **formalist-substantivist debate** is one such example. The **formalist** position is based on economic assumptions, which state that all people are rational, logical decision makers. Since all resources are scarce, all people will behave in a universal way: they will consider the costs, benefits, time, and energy required for an action, and they behave in a way that is the most beneficial to themselves. The **substantivists** argue that decision making is based on the norms and values of each culture. What is rational and beneficial for one person may be different for someone of another culture. Anthropologists have identified some patterns related to human economic behavior (decision making), which are also tied into subsistence strategies, political organization, and social organization.

Subsistence and Settlement Patterns

To begin untangling some of the complexities, anthropologists start with identifying **subsistence strategies**: the ways people survive in their physical environment (foraging, pastoralism, horticulture, and agriculture). These strategies tend to support a certain **population size** based on if and where they **settle** (live) as a group. Research also suggests that other patterns relating to property ownership and land management are related to certain subsistence strategies.

Foraging

Foraging is collecting plants, fishing, and hunting animals in order to survive. The majority of food comes from foraging for plants, nuts, fruits, and vegetables. Foragers are able to identify a large number of plants and animals. Foragers move from place to place as the seasons change, vegetation dies and grows, and animals move. Since foragers must carry all of their belonging as they move, they tend to have few material possessions. Foragers use simple tools such as spears, digging sticks, and bows and arrows.

Pastoralism

Pastoralism is caring for and keeping herds of domesticated animals, such as goats, cattle, or camels. Some pastoralists move their animals throughout the seasons to areas where there are enough pastures for the herd. They leave behind people at the permanent village. In other types of pastoralist cultures, everyone moves with the herds. There are no permanent settlements. Pastoralists take care to eat or sell only the animals they can spare—they must maintain enough breeding stock throughout the year. Their diets often include the blood and milk of the animal because the animal does not have to be killed to use these resources. Pastoralists will also trade with neighbors for other food and materials they may need.

Horticulture

Horticulture is growing and cultivating crops with simple hand tools, such as digging sticks or hoes. Horticulturalists who live in tropical forests practice swidden farming (also known as slash-and-burn cultivation). In swidden farming, trees and plants in a specific area are cut down and then burned. Crops are planted in the ashes, which act as fertilizer. Horticulture can support villages of 100 to 1,000 people. These villages will also supplement their diet by hunting, fishing, or raising a few animals. There is a sense that the village gardens are **communal property** because the crops are dedicated to feeding and maintaining the group as a whole.

Agriculture

Agriculture is the deliberate production of food by growing crops and tending animals. Hand plows or plows pulled by animals, irrigation, and long-term breeding of livestock are all characteristic of this subsistence strategy. The methods lead to a surplus of food and animal resources, which then can be traded or sold. The idea of **private property** and ownership becomes more prevalent as people farm and claim lands as their own, which are then transferred to the next generation in the family. A steady supply of food transforms small villages into larger towns. As technology improves, agriculture becomes even more productive. Farmland could now support larger city centers and then states. Since food is available for purchase, people can specialize in other occupations. Governments emerge to manage the needs of the large populace. Social hierarchies allow people to experience unequal access to important resources (social stratification).

Industrialism

Few people, compared to the rest of the population, are involved with food production. Instead of selling food or goods they have produced themselves, people are selling their labor and working for others. Laborers earn wages in order to purchase goods, services, and food.

Economic Systems

Economic systems are the cultural norms and values that regulate the production, allocation, and consumption of goods and services. For **production**, each society has a **division of labor**: the person or group responsible for completing particular tasks. Generally in a foraging society, women tend to gather and men tend to hunt. In large-scale agricultural societies, the owners of the land and tools are separate from those who actually cultivate, grow, and harvest the crops.

Societies also **allocate** (distribute) and **consume** (use) goods and services in specific ways. People engage in **reciprocity** when they exchange goods and services that are of roughly equal value. For example, foragers will, over time, give one another food resources to maintain and preserve social ties. **Redistribution** occurs when goods are collected by a central person or office and then reallocated into the society. In industrialized societies, for example, a government collects taxes and returns them to the populace in the form of national health care, education, etc. In a **market exchange**, the buying and selling of goods and services are dependent upon how many of those goods and services exist and how many people need or want those things.

Political Organizations

Subsistence strategies and economic systems are also related to **political organization**: the ways in which societies maintain social order. Whether maintaining **customs** (traditional behaviors) or punishing the violation of formal codes of conduct **(laws)**, political organizations regulate behavior for social cohesion. **Political associations** are often categorized as bands, tribes, chiefdoms, or states.

- **Bands** are small groups of people with no formal leadership. Foraging groups tend to live in bands and function through group consensus.
- A **tribe**, which is usually found in pastoralist or horticulturalist culture, is made up of groups related by kinship or family ties. These groups may believe they are descended from a common ancestor. Tribes may have leaders but these are informal positions based on prestige or popularity among people. Some anthropologists argue that tribes are more likely to engage in **war** (deliberate acts of violence between groups of people) although the reason why is unclear.
- **Chiefdoms** are ruled by a chief who collects and redistributes goods among the people. Chiefdoms are hierarchical and the leader controls the economic activities of the group (which are usually highly productive horticulturalists or pastoralists).
- In state societies, **governments** are the social structures that manage the society's territory, redistribute goods, manage services, maintain infrastructure, and keep law and order.

These modern political systems of government can take several forms and variations, including **democracies** (where all members of a state system make decisions about state affairs), **oligarchies** (where power and decision making lie in the hands of a powerful few), or **autocracies** (where a single person holds all power).

While foraging, pastoralism, horticulture, agriculture, industrialism and the various types of political organizations still exist in the present day, anthropologists study how these systems are changing and adapting. **Globalization** (the increasing interconnectedness of people around the world), for example, is closely examined in relationship to the environment. As more countries turn to industrialism and increased trade with one another, what is the environmental impact? How have cultures around the world dealt with these changes?

Anthropologists are also studying how economic and political organizations have changed over time as a result of **colonialism**: foreign powers establishing colonies and outposts in other countries, usually for the exploitation of people and resources. Specifically, the expansion of European powers throughout the world from approximately the fifteenth to the middle of the twentieth century is described as one of the catalysts for emergence of the **world system theory** (developed by Immanuel Wallerstein). Core countries, many of whose wealth and power were developed during the colonial era, continue dominating the world economic system by exploiting peripheral societies (usually poorer countries). For example, anthropologists study global powers like the European Union and its reliance on the labor of countries like the Philippines and Vietnam to produce inexpensive goods.

Groups and Associations

Cultural norms and values influence how people willingly associate or are unwillingly grouped together in other ways besides kinship. People may choose to come together for a specific purpose or because they share common interests (**associations**). Occupation associations (such as doctors' groups) or recreation groups (such as sports clubs) are examples of people voluntarily grouping themselves. Another example, grouping by **age**, means that in a society people of the same age experience culturally relevant experiences at the same time.

RELIGION

Belief Systems

Each culture shares a **worldview**: a broad set of ideas and beliefs about the nature of their reality. Part of that worldview is **religion**, an organized set of beliefs and practices related to the supernatural. **Spirituality** (sometimes defined separately from religion) refers to an individual's beliefs about the supernatural; participation in an organized religious group is not a necessary part of that belief. When religion begins to disappear from a group's worldview, this is described as **secularization**. People who self-identify as spiritual, for example, may group together through **informal organizations** to discuss their ideas. There may be no specific structure or set of rules to adhere to.

Anthropologists once believed that all religions passed through stages, starting with **animism** (the belief that everything is made of spirits or supernatural energies), then **polytheism** (the belief in many divine beings), and finally **monotheism** (the belief in a single divine being). Anthropologists no longer support the idea of stages and recognize that religion encompasses a wide range of beliefs, ideas, and practices. Anthropologists now try to identify patterns that emerge through the study of religions.

All religions have some sort of **sacred narrative** (or **myth**): sacred stories that explain the relationship between the supernatural and reality. For believers, these narratives are important for how the group functions and what they believe. Religious groups likely use symbols, such as religious pendants or masks used in rituals. Supernatural beings in religious practice include spirits, divine beings (for example gods and goddesses), or **ancestor spirits** (spirits who are relatives or kin to the group). Some religious groups believe ancestral spirits bind them together as one people and, as a result, have a special relationship with an animal, plant, or other objects that represents that spirit (**totemism**).

Religious Practices and Rituals

Religious practitioners are specialists in the religious group who carry out any number of duties. **Priestesses** and **priests** hold a full-time position in the group and are expected to conduct rituals, interact with the supernatural, and lead the community. **Shamans** are often **healers**, people who treat and cure medical and spiritual illnesses. Shamans can enter altered states of consciousness through rituals or by other means and communicate with the world of the supernatural.

Rituals, ceremonial acts designed for use during specific occasions, are also an important part of religious life. **Rites of passage** are rituals that mark an individual's movement from one social status or stage of life to another. These include ceremonies for birth, marriage, aging, and death. **Rites of purification** ritually cleanse a person or group when a taboo has been violated. **Rites of intensification** bind a group together and reinforce the norms and values of that group.

Some rituals involve **magic**: rituals involving actions (verbal, physical, and/or written) invoking supernatural power to try and effect some sort of change. **Imitative** or **sympathetic magic** is the

belief that something that happens in a ritual will cause the same thing to happen outside the ritual. To harm a person, for example, someone might ritually harm a doll that is supposed to represent that person. **Contagious magic** is the idea that something keeps a connection with an object or person it was once in contact with. **Witchcraft** refers to magical rituals used to cause harm.

Other rituals include **prayer**: appeals to the supernatural. **Sacrifice** is an offering to supernatural beings to demonstrate faith and loyalty. Somewhat related to the idea of sacrifice is **pilgrimage**, traveling to a sacred site to prove one's dedication to the faith. **Divination** is a ritual that tries to discover hidden information or find lost people or objects.

Religious groups are also subject to cultural change. In response to great social changes and high levels of stress or unhappiness, **revitalization movements** may emerge. These movements promise widespread reforms, based on religious beliefs, which will improve life and end suffering. Some movements are **messianic**, believing that an individual will change the world into paradise. Other movements are **millenarian**, believing that a catastrophe will occur that will destroy most of the world but will eventually lead to heaven on earth. In response to culture change that brings two or more religious faiths together, **syncretism** sometimes occurs: the merging of two or more religions into a new faith.

MODERNIZATION AND APPLICATION

Applied Anthropology

While anthropology is typically divided into the four subfields we have just reviewed (physical anthropology, linguistics, cultural anthropology, and archaeology), anthropologists are debating the inclusion of a fifth subdiscipline: **applied anthropology**. What is applied anthropology? This subdiscipline uses the perspective and tools of physical, archaeological, linguistic, and cultural anthropology to solve a variety of problems. In 1941, the Society for Applied Anthropology was founded. During World War II, anthropologists such as Margaret Mead, Ruth Benedict, and George Murdock used their training to support the United States war effort. Today, anthropologists can be found conducting research in many different contexts.

For example, physical anthropologists often use their skills to conduct **forensic anthropology**, the analysis of skeletal remains. These remains may be part of an FBI or police investigation, and careful examination can provide the clues necessary to help solve a case. Nongovernment organizations wanting to identify the human remains found at a mass grave after wartime might employ a physical anthropologist to help with that work as well.

Some archaeologists choose to work in the field of **cultural resource management (CRM)**. Many countries and businesses around the world hire archaeologists to examine cultural remains in a variety of contexts. For example, say a construction company in San Francisco, California, has torn down a building and is preparing the ground for new development. If, during the course of the digging, construction workers come across any artifacts and/or human remains, they are legally required to call an archaeologist to the site. The archaeologists and their team will examine what has been found and will decide how to proceed. The artifacts may be excavated and studied or reburied, for example.

Linguistic anthropologists may work with a group of people whose language is in danger of dying out. Linguists can help with writing a dictionary, recording the grammar and syntax of the language and help the community preserve their heritage (also referred to as **cultural preservation**). In another example, linguistic anthropologists might develop programs to help multilingual students succeed in school.

Cultural anthropologists use their skills in many situations, from the medical field to large corporations to nongovernment organizations. Computer companies, for example, hire cultural anthropologists to design and carry out specific research projects. A laptop designer may want to know what sort of features to include in the equipment. An anthropologist who is used to living and working with the community might decide to spend time on a boat with deep sea fishermen. He or she could observe and speak with the captain and crew to figure out how they use their computers and what would be the most useful upgrades. In another example, an anthropologist might work as liaison between a shaman and Western-trained medical doctors to provide medical care to a community.

Cultural Change and the Future

Anthropologists from across the subdisciplines are also working with nongovernment organizations, government offices, human rights groups, and others to help insure that indigenous people have the power to represent their own interests. Historically, governments have been the cause of **directed cultural change**, which often forced people (indigenous Americans First-Nations or the Ju/'hoansi of southern African, for example) to give up their lands and cultures to satisfy territorial expansion. When possible, anthropologists have tried to aid indigenous groups if they request it and in ways that preserve the choices and dignity of those groups. All over the world, as culture change continues and globalization tightens connections between people and places, indigenous groups fight for **cultural survival**: the right to preserve, remember, and celebrate one's culture.

Anthropologists are also asked to consider future directions for research: specifically, what problems or challenges are in store for humans? Anthropologists continue studying the relationship between the environment and people, for example, to determine how cross-cultural responses to climate change may offer solutions to human survival. Other serious questions pose significant challenges. In light of globalization, for example, anthropologists consider if people from around the world are embracing a global culture of shared beliefs, behaviors, norms, and values. If so, what is that culture? What impact would such a culture have upon indigenous survival as historically subjugated groups fight to maintain their cultural heritage? What role can and should anthropology play in addressing current and future challenges?

SUMMING IT UP

- **Anthropology** studies the human existence via four major subdisciplines: **physical anthropology**, **archaeology**, **cultural anthropology**, and **linguistic anthropology**. Anthropologists also debate the inclusion of a fifth subdiscipline: **applied anthropology**. The holistic perspective of anthropology strives to understand the totality of human existence and how different components (cultural, biological, material, etc.) interact with one another.

- Charles Darwin's evolutionary theory of **natural selection** states every species of life exhibits a range of variation that helps it survive and reproduce or die in its environment. Gregor Mendel then explained how these traits are passed to offspring by identifying specific traits of plants and how these traits were (or were not) passed along from one generation to the next.

- Genes are the blueprints for making proteins, which maintain the human body and cause people to have different traits such as eye or hair color and blood type. Genes may cause more than one version of a particular trait (such as blue eyes or brown eyes, or tall vs. short), referred to as **alleles** of a gene. **Mendel's Principles of Inheritance** are the principle of segregation (each organism usually has two alleles of each gene, and offspring will receive one allele of each gene from each parent); the principle of dominance (one allele will dominate over the other); and the principle of independent assortment (genes for different traits are inherited independently of one another).

- Genetic variations in a species are the **gene pool**. Evolution refers to how the frequency of alleles in the gene pool changes over time. Changes are summarized by **the four forces of evolution**: mutation (random changes in DNA); **genetic drift** (when random events cause an individual to die without reproducing, eradicating a genotype from the gene pool); **gene flow** (when an individual or individuals from one gene pool introduces genetic material to another gene pool through producing offspring); and natural selection (the survival of individuals with traits that are best adapted to their environment).

- **Primatologists** study how living primates such as gorillas and chimpanzees have adapted over time to help us understand how humans may have changed over the millennia. Primatologists study feces, hair, and teeth for clues about diet. They try to determine how primates have evolved in response to environmental pressures and compare results with research conducted with humans to understand how much behavior is driven by nature and how much is driven by nurture.

- A **paleoanthropologist** studies fossil records to learn about the ancestors and relatives of *Homo sapiens*. Paleoanthropologists can attempt to find a fossil's age through relative dating (determining whether a fossil is older or younger than another fossil, sometimes by its placement within the ground) and absolute dating (its age in absolute years, sometimes found by carbon-14 dating).

- **Archaeologists** study prehistoric and historic human cultures based on their material remains. Archaeologists' research helps us understand human biology by determining how we physically interact with the world around us. They categorize the human past based on the type of tools used by our ancestors.

- During the **Paleolithic era**, humans survived by foraging and lived in small groups that moved from place to place due to environmental changes. In the **Neolithic era**, agriculture emerged in many cultures around the world, with most changes occurring 12,000 to 10,000 years ago. Transition from foraging to agriculture meant that people could stay in one place. This led villages to turn into towns, with farmlands supporting bigger city centers. Then, governments emerged to manage the needs of the large populace.

- **Linguistic anthropology** is the study of human language: a system that allows humans to communicate information and discuss events that occurred in the past, are happening in the present, or could happen in the future. **Descriptive** or **structural linguistics** examines the construction of languages; **historical linguistics** studies the connection between languages and how they change over time; **sociolinguistics** studies verbal and nonverbal communication in a variety of social contexts: the relationship between culture and language.

- **Cultural anthropology** focuses on researching and comparing patterns of human cultural diversity. The process of learning to be part of a cultural group through observation of the world and people around us is called **enculturation**. Anthropologists recognize many different aspects of culture, including economic systems, political organizations, and religions. Anthropologists study how well (or poorly) these systems integrate and function together. Human culture evolves to give people a better chance to survive and reproduce in their environment. Cultures change at different speeds from one another due to environmental pressures, disease, natural disasters, conflict within the group or from outside of the group, among other reasons. Cultures may also change due to invention, innovation, and diffusion.

- A cultural anthropologist, also known as an **ethnographer**, may decide to focus on a specific culture: a group that shares behavioral patterns, values, and norms. Anthropologists ask questions about society—a group of people who usually share the same culture, live in a specific territory, and share common goals. Anthropologists focus on the **emic** perspective: the point of view of the person who is part of that cultural group, and then often write an **ethnography** with detailed descriptions of that culture from the **etic** perspective: the point of view of someone who is outside of that cultural group.

- Anthropologists argue against **ethnocentrism**, the belief that one's own norms and values are the only correct standard for living and should be used to judge others. **Cultural relativism** argues that each culture must be understood by its own norms and values and not be immediately judged by the standards of other cultures.

- Lewis Henry Morgan and Edward Burnett Tylor were the chief authors of the theory of **cultural evolution**. They argued that every cultural group in the world should evolve through three stages: savagery, barbarism, and civilization; their ethnocentric perspective stated Western society was the most evolved and therefore the highest standard everyone should aspire to. Franz Boas conducted research among the North American Inuit on Baffin Island. He determined cultures should be understood by their own internal norms and values, and his research influenced the discipline's rejection of ethnocentrism and cultural evolution. It focused on cultural relativism and cultural determinism (how culture shapes an individual's personality). Bronislaw Malinowski pioneered the core anthropological method of participant observation and determined through research that cultural groups must be understood by their own internal logics.

- In the **formalist-substantivist debate**, the formalist position assumes people make rational decisions and will consider the costs, benefits, time, and energy to behave in a way beneficial to themselves. **Substantivists** argue that decision making is based on the norms and values of each culture. **Subsistence strategies** are the ways people survive in their physical environment and include foraging, pastoralism, horticulture, and agriculture.

- Economic systems are the cultural norms and values that regulate the production, allocation, and consumption of goods and services. Each society has a **division of labor**: the person or group responsible for completing particular tasks. People engage in **reciprocity** when they exchange goods and services that are of roughly equal value. **Redistribution** occurs when goods are collected by a central person or office and then reallocated into the society. In a **market exchange**, the buying and selling of goods and services are dependent upon the number of goods and services and the demand for them.

- **Political organizations** maintain social order in a society; they regulate behavior for social cohesion. **Political associations** are often categorized as bands (groups with no formal leadership), tribes (groups related by kinship or family ties), chiefdoms (ruled by a chief who collects and redistributes goods among the people), or states (run by governments that manage services and keep law and order).

- In **egalitarian** societies, all people have about the same access to goods and services, wealth, status, and power. In **rank** societies, some have a higher status than others, but everyone still has the same access to goods and services, wealth, status, and power. In **stratified** societies, different levels have unequal access to goods and services, wealth, status, and power. In an **open class system**, there is a possibility of moving between the different levels of a social hierarchy. In a **closed class system**, there is no possibility of moving between the different levels of a social hierarchy.

- **Marriage** is a cultural institution that defines the parameters of a union between 2 or more people, establishes rules for the responsibility of children, and clarifies the relationship between the kin of the married people. Culturally based rules require people marry within their own group (**endogamy**) or outside their own group (**exogamy**). Culture defines both marriage and family.

- **Descent** is how a culture defines how individuals are related to their parents. In **bilateral descent**, descent is traced through both the paternal (father's) and maternal (mother's) lines. In **unilateral descent**, descent is traced through either the **patrilineal** (male) or **matrilineal** (female) line. **Kinship** refers to a network of relatives related by blood or marriage, and **kinship systems** are the ways in which a cultural group classify how people are related to one another.

- **Sex** refers to the genetic combination of X and Y chromosomes. **Gender** commonly refers to the cultural norms, values, expectations, and categories of what is "masculine" and "feminine." Gender male or female does not always correspond to sex male or sex female.

- **Race** refers to certain physical traits grouped together under specific labels and categories. Though genetic testing identifies a single human species, over time the idea that humans were separate "races" became accepted as natural and correct. Although "race" does not exist biologically, it is still used to justify social stratification.

- **Religion** is an organized set of beliefs and practices related to the supernatural. **Spirituality** refers to an individual's beliefs about the supernatural. Anthropologists believe religion encompasses a wide range of beliefs, ideas, and practices and try to identify patterns that emerge through the study of religions. Religious groups are subject to cultural change.

- **Applied anthropology** uses the perspective and tools of physical, archaeo-logical, linguistic, and cultural anthropology to solve problems. For example, **physical anthropologists** often use their skills to conduct forensic anthropol-ogy for FBI or police investigations. Some **archaeologists** work in **cultural resource management (CRM)**, in which countries and businesses around the world hire archaeologists to examine cultural remains in a variety of contexts. **Linguistic anthropologists** might develop programs to help multi-lingual students succeed in school. All over the world, as indigenous groups fight for the right to preserve their culture, **cultural anthropologists** can be called upon to aid their cause.

Chapter 4

General Anthropology Post-Test

POST-TEST ANSWER SHEET

1. Ⓐ Ⓑ Ⓒ Ⓓ	17. Ⓐ Ⓑ Ⓒ Ⓓ	33. Ⓐ Ⓑ Ⓒ Ⓓ
2. Ⓐ Ⓑ Ⓒ Ⓓ	18. Ⓐ Ⓑ Ⓒ Ⓓ	34. Ⓐ Ⓑ Ⓒ Ⓓ
3. Ⓐ Ⓑ Ⓒ Ⓓ	19. Ⓐ Ⓑ Ⓒ Ⓓ	35. Ⓐ Ⓑ Ⓒ Ⓓ
4. Ⓐ Ⓑ Ⓒ Ⓓ	20. Ⓐ Ⓑ Ⓒ Ⓓ	36. Ⓐ Ⓑ Ⓒ Ⓓ
5. Ⓐ Ⓑ Ⓒ Ⓓ	21. Ⓐ Ⓑ Ⓒ Ⓓ	37. Ⓐ Ⓑ Ⓒ Ⓓ
6. Ⓐ Ⓑ Ⓒ Ⓓ	22. Ⓐ Ⓑ Ⓒ Ⓓ	38. Ⓐ Ⓑ Ⓒ Ⓓ
7. Ⓐ Ⓑ Ⓒ Ⓓ	23. Ⓐ Ⓑ Ⓒ Ⓓ	39. Ⓐ Ⓑ Ⓒ Ⓓ
8. Ⓐ Ⓑ Ⓒ Ⓓ	24. Ⓐ Ⓑ Ⓒ Ⓓ	40. Ⓐ Ⓑ Ⓒ Ⓓ
9. Ⓐ Ⓑ Ⓒ Ⓓ	25. Ⓐ Ⓑ Ⓒ Ⓓ	41. Ⓐ Ⓑ Ⓒ Ⓓ
10. Ⓐ Ⓑ Ⓒ Ⓓ	26. Ⓐ Ⓑ Ⓒ Ⓓ	42. Ⓐ Ⓑ Ⓒ Ⓓ
11. Ⓐ Ⓑ Ⓒ Ⓓ	27. Ⓐ Ⓑ Ⓒ Ⓓ	43. Ⓐ Ⓑ Ⓒ Ⓓ
12. Ⓐ Ⓑ Ⓒ Ⓓ	28. Ⓐ Ⓑ Ⓒ Ⓓ	44. Ⓐ Ⓑ Ⓒ Ⓓ
13. Ⓐ Ⓑ Ⓒ Ⓓ	29. Ⓐ Ⓑ Ⓒ Ⓓ	45. Ⓐ Ⓑ Ⓒ Ⓓ
14. Ⓐ Ⓑ Ⓒ Ⓓ	30. Ⓐ Ⓑ Ⓒ Ⓓ	46. Ⓐ Ⓑ Ⓒ Ⓓ
15. Ⓐ Ⓑ Ⓒ Ⓓ	31. Ⓐ Ⓑ Ⓒ Ⓓ	47. Ⓐ Ⓑ Ⓒ Ⓓ
16. Ⓐ Ⓑ Ⓒ Ⓓ	32. Ⓐ Ⓑ Ⓒ Ⓓ	48. Ⓐ Ⓑ Ⓒ Ⓓ

49. Ⓐ Ⓑ Ⓒ Ⓓ   53. Ⓐ Ⓑ Ⓒ Ⓓ   57. Ⓐ Ⓑ Ⓒ Ⓓ

50. Ⓐ Ⓑ Ⓒ Ⓓ   54. Ⓐ Ⓑ Ⓒ Ⓓ   58. Ⓐ Ⓑ Ⓒ Ⓓ

51. Ⓐ Ⓑ Ⓒ Ⓓ   55. Ⓐ Ⓑ Ⓒ Ⓓ   59. Ⓐ Ⓑ Ⓒ Ⓓ

52. Ⓐ Ⓑ Ⓒ Ⓓ   56. Ⓐ Ⓑ Ⓒ Ⓓ   60. Ⓐ Ⓑ Ⓒ Ⓓ

GENERAL ANTHROPOLOGY POST-TEST

Directions: Carefully read each of the following 60 questions. Choose the best answer to each question and fill in the corresponding circle on the answer sheet. The Answer Key and Explanations can be found following this post-test.

1. Which subfield of physical anthropology reconstructs humanity's evolutionary past using the fossil record?

    A. Paleoanthropology
    B. Primatology
    C. Human variation
    D. Forensic anthropology

2. Whose theory of evolution by natural selection revolutionized the field of biology?

    A. Gregor Mendel
    B. Charles Darwin
    C. Franz Boas
    D. Bronislaw Malinowski

3. Prehistoric archaeology studies artifacts from which time period?

    A. Dating from 10 to 50 years old
    B. Dating from 100 to 500 years old
    C. Dating from 1,000 to 5,000 years old
    D. Dating from 10,000 to 50,000 years old

4. The theory of Structuralism is associated with which anthropologist?

    A. E.O. Wilson
    B. Bronislaw Malinowksi
    C. Ruth Benedict
    D. Claude Lévi-Strauss

5. A _____ is something that represents something else.

A. syntax
B. symbol
C. grammar
D. phonology

6. The Neolithic Revolution refers to

A. the extinction of *Homo neanderthalensis.*
B. the production of pottery.
C. the emergence of agriculture.
D. the earliest expression of human imagination through cave art.

7. Which primates are generally solitary creatures who tend to forage for food over broad areas?

A. Gorillas
B. Bonobos
C. Chimpanzees
D. Orangutans

8. Ethnography is best described as

A. the science of observing people in a laboratory setting.
B. a list of the number of people who live in a particular city.
C. a written account of an anthropologist's fieldwork and research.
D. a collection of newspaper articles about a cultural group.

9. Franz Boas's Historical Particularism was developed as a critique of which theory?

A. Cultural Evolution
B. The Four Forces of Evolution
C. Neo-evolutionary Thought
D. Cultural Relativism

10. Cultural determinism argues that

A. one's own cultural norms are the only correct standard for living and should be used to judge others.
B. culture moves through the three stages of savagery, barbarism, and civilization.
C. culture shapes an individual's personality.
D. culture is transmitted through genes.

11. A group may claim it holds certain cultural norms and values. However, those norms and values are not necessarily acted out in reality. This is best described as a tension between

    A. symbolic and nonsymbolic culture.
    B. adaptive and nonadaptive culture.
    C. shared and learned culture.
    D. real and ideal culture.

12. The emic perspective refers to

    A. the point of view of someone outside of a cultural group.
    B. the point of view of someone who is part of a cultural group.
    C. a religious world view.
    D. a secular world view.

13. Why do members of foraging groups own very few material possessions?

    A. Foragers are mostly interested in collecting vegetables, not material possessions.
    B. Foragers must carry all of their belongings as they move; lighter is better.
    C. Foragers share all possessions among the group.
    D. Foragers do not use tools.

14. Descent traced through either the patrilineal or matrilineal line is referred to as

    A. unilateral descent.
    B. bilateral descent.
    C. phratry.
    D. moiety.

15. What is an open class system?

    A. A society of relative equals
    B. A society of chiefs and commoners
    C. Stratified systems where there is a possibility of moving between the different levels of a social hierarchy
    D. Stratified systems where there is no possibility of moving between the different levels of a social hierarchy

16. Which anthropologist will be contacted if a shipwreck is discovered while an area is being prepared to construct a new building?

    A. Physical anthropologist
    B. Archaeologist
    C. Linguist
    D. Cultural anthropologist

17. What is a genotype?

    A. Genes and alleles each person possesses
    B. When one allele dominates over the other
    C. The four forces of evolution
    D. A numeric classification system for fossils

18. *Australopithecus afarensis'* most distinguishing feature is that it

    A. had human-like facial features.
    B. was bipedal.
    C. invented the wheel.
    D. existed at the same time as the dinosaurs.

19. Which subsistence strategy did humans rely on during the Paleolithic era?

    A. Agriculture
    B. Pastoralism
    C. Horticulture
    D. Foraging

20. What was the main reason Cultural Evolution was discredited as a theory?

    A. Morgan and Tylor were too biased as participant observers during fieldwork.
    B. The "industrial" stage was missing from "savagery," "barbarism," and "civilization."
    C. Morgan and Tylor gathered demographic data from Europe rather than the Americas.
    D. Cross-cultural comparisons support the idea that cultures change and innovate at their own pace.

21. An anthropologist who is interested in researching cultural universals might use which method?

   A. Ethnology
   B. Observation
   C. Interviewing
   D. Absolute dating

22. In the substantivist-formalist debates, the formalist argument is based on what assumption?

   A. People are rational, logical decision makers.
   B. People place the group's needs above their own.
   C. People are irrational, illogical decision makers.
   D. People place the needs of the family above their own.

23. Who are the Hijra?

   A. A pastoralist group in Nigeria
   B. A third gender in India
   C. A fourth gender in the Philippines
   D. A horticultural group in Vietnam

24. Within the subdiscipline of physical anthropology, primatology refers to

   A. research of primal foraging societies.
   B. cataloging the first fossils of *Homo sapiens* ancestors.
   C. the study of primordial cell development.
   D. the biological research and observation of nonhuman primates.

25. Why are prehistoric archaeologists interested in sites where *Homo habilis* has been discovered?

   A. Some *Homo habilis* sites contain Mousterian stone tools that are some of the earliest examples of human culture.
   B. Oldowan stone tools, some of the earliest evidence of tool making, have been discovered with *Homo habilis*.
   C. *Homo habilis* traded pottery with *Homo sapiens*.
   D. Evidence of intensive food production has been found with *Homo habilis*.

26. Anthropologist Marvin Harris studied the sacred cattle of India and proposed which theory?

   A. Cognitive Anthropology
   B. Ecological Materialism
   C. Functionalism
   D. Sociobiology

27. Diffusion drives culture change because

   A. it speeds up cultural evolution.
   B. culture contact leads people to become less innovative.
   C. ideas are forgotten, and people need to invent new technologies.
   D. new ideas, devices, and/or innovations often spread from one culture to another.

28. What are some ways societies maintain social control?

   A. Invention and innovation
   B. Foraging and agriculture
   C. Laws and customs
   D. Participant observation and interviewing

29. *Kinship* is best defined as

   A. a lineage.
   B. maternal and paternal blood relatives.
   C. a network of relatives related by blood or marriage.
   D. specific ways relatives are labeled or referred to.

30. What are sacred narratives?

   A. Myths that are inherently false
   B. Rituals invoking supernatural power to effect change
   C. Stories that explain the relationship between the supernatural and reality
   D. Rituals that try to discover hidden information or find lost people or objects

31. Which anthropologist will use his or her skills to conduct cultural resource management?

   A. Historical linguist
   B. Paleoanthropologist
   C. Archaeologist
   D. Ethnographer

32. A religious group's weekly prayer meetings are best described as a rite of

   A. passage.
   B. purification.
   C. intensification.
   D. syncretism.

33. Ascribed status is usually central to which type of society?

   A. Monogamous
   B. Polygamous
   C. Open class system
   D. Closed class system

34. What is a division of labor?

   A. The number of hours in a work day
   B. Different salaries for different types of jobs
   C. The person or group responsible for completing particular tasks
   D. Tasks that should be completed in a certain order

35. A _____ revitalization movement believes that an individual will change the world into paradise.

   A. messianic
   B. millenarian
   C. totemic
   D. secularization

36. The practice of comparing and contrasting the cultural patterns of one group with other ethnographic examples is referred to as

   A. ethnographer.
   B. ethnography.
   C. ethnology.
   D. ethnomusicology.

37. Magic, divination, and sacrifice are examples of

A. myth.
B. rituals.
C. exogamy.
D. reciprocity.

38. What is cultural survival?

A. Another term for cultural universal
B. Artifacts from early human cultures
C. The right to preserve, remember, and celebrate one's culture
D. Historic records

39. Which anthropologist would be the most interested in how languages have changed over time?

A. Structural linguist
B. Cultural anthropologist
C. Historical linguist
D. Historic archaeologist

40. Which human ancestor is associated with Acheulean stone tools?

A. *Australopithecus afarensis*
B. *Homo habilis*
C. *Homo erectus*
D. *Homo neanderthalensis*

41. The belief that everything is made of spirits or supernatural energies is referred to as

A. sacrifice.
B. witchcraft.
C. syncretism.
D. animism.

42. Which anthropologist would be most interested in researching how different genders speak with one another at the workplace?

A. Historical linguist
B. Descriptive linguist
C. Sociolinguist
D. Structural linguist

43. Primatologists observe and study nonhuman primates because

    A. chimpanzee DNA is the same as 50 percent of human DNA.
    B. unlike humans, orangutans do not know how to use tools.
    C. gorillas can help us understand how humans may have evolved over the millennia.
    D. meerkats display human-like behavior.

44. Franz Boas and Bronislaw Malinowski advocated for which method to be at the center of anthropological fieldwork?

    A. Absolute dating
    B. Relative dating
    C. Participant observation
    D. Armchair anthropology

45. Which phrase accurately describes "culture"?

    A. A group who shares values and norms
    B. A group who lives in a specific territory
    C. An individual's personality
    D. An individual's belief system

46. _____ occurs when goods are collected by a central person or office and then reallocated into society.

    A. Production
    B. Market exchange
    C. Reciprocity
    D. Redistribution

47. The emergence of social stratification is directly related to

    A. agriculture.
    B. tool use.
    C. cave art.
    D. migration.

48. Which is an example of relative dating?

    A. Stratigraphy
    B. Radiocarbon dating
    C. Dendrochronology
    D. Potassium-argon dating

49. Art is broadly defined as expression of the human imagination. The earliest form of human art, cave drawings, date back to which era?

   A. Lower Paleolithic
   B. Middle Paleolithic
   C. Upper Paleolithic
   D. Neolithic

50. Which anthropologist will use his or her skills to conduct forensic anthropology?

   A. Primatologist
   B. Cultural anthropologist
   C. Linguist
   D. Physical anthropologist

51. From an anthropological perspective what is a pilgrimage?

   A. A religious movement that promises widespread reform
   B. Traveling for tourism
   C. Migrating to a new country
   D. Traveling to a sacred site to prove one's dedication to the faith

52. Which anthropologist could conduct participant observation among computer gamers to research their preferences in personal computing hardware?

   A. Maritime archaeologist
   B. Primatologist
   C. Forensic anthropologist
   D. Cultural anthropologist

53. The physical expression of the genotype refers to

   A. DNA.
   B. genes.
   C. allele.
   D. phenotype.

54. What is directed culture change?

A. When elites devise and enforce plans that force the less powerful to accept changes

B. One of the forces of cultural evolution

C. The practice of witchcraft to harm others

D. Evidence of totemism among a religious group

55. Political associations are important because they

A. organize voting.

B. help maintain social order.

C. led the Neolithic Revolution.

D. moderated the formalist and substantivist debate.

56. In anthropological studies, domestication is best described as

A. humans making stone tools.

B. fieldwork conducted in the United States.

C. women staying close to home to raise children.

D. humans guiding the growth of plants and the reproduction of animals.

57. Individuals are said to be better adapted to the environment they live in if they are able to

A. live past the age of 5.

B. live to the age of 100.

C. prepare for natural disasters.

D. survive and reproduce.

58. The idea of cultural relativism developed out of which theoretical framework?

A. Sociobiology

B. Structuralism

C. Historical particularism

D. Anthropology and gender

59. After marriage, spouses live separately from their parents in their own household. What is the anthropological term for this type of residence?

    A. Neolocal
    B. Bilocal
    C. Avunculocal
    D. Ambilocal

60. What is an example of directed culture change?

    A. Random changes in DNA that may lead to beneficial, harmful, or neutral traits for an organism
    B. Events such as an earthquake that cause an individual to die without reproducing
    C. Understanding how different cultural components work with one another
    D. Indigenous people being forced to give up land to colonizers.

ANSWER KEY AND EXPLANATIONS

1. A	13. B	25. B	37. B	49. C
2. B	14. A	26. B	38. C	50. D
3. D	15. C	27. D	39. C	51. D
4. D	16. B	28. C	40. C	52. D
5. B	17. A	29. C	41. D	53. D
6. C	18. B	30. C	42. C	54. A
7. D	19. D	31. C	43. C	55. B
8. C	20. D	32. C	44. C	56. D
9. A	21. A	33. D	45. A	57. D
10. C	22. A	34. C	46. D	58. C
11. D	23. B	35. A	47. A	59. A
12. B	24. D	36. C	48. A	60. D

1. **The correct answer is A.** Paleoanthropology reconstructs humanity's evolutionary past through the fossil record. Choice B is incorrect because primatology is the biological research and observation of nonhuman primates to shed light on human evolution. Choice C is incorrect because human variation is the study of biological differences (physiology, genetics, etc.) within the human species. Choice D is incorrect because forensic anthropology is the analysis of skeletal remains as part of a formal investigation (for the police, the FBI, etc.).

2. **The correct answer is B.** Charles Darwin proposed the theory of evolution by natural selection in the mid-1800s. Gregor Mendel, choice A, is incorrect because his work was the basis of Mendel's Principles of Inheritance. Choices C and D are incorrect because Boas and Malinowski were scientists who revolutionized the field of anthropology.

3. **The correct answer is D.** Prehistoric archaeology focuses on human culture prior to written historical records. The late Neolithic period, which dates to 10,000 to 50,000 years ago, marks the end of the prehistoric era. Choices A, B, and C are incorrect because the artifacts that old would date from the historic era (when writing and record keeping emerged).

4. The correct answer is D. Claude Lévi-Strauss is the anthropologist who established the theory of Structuralism. Choice A is incorrect because E.O. Wilson is associated with the Sociobiology theoretical school. Choice B is incorrect because Bronislaw Malinowksi is associated with the theory of Functionalism. Choice C is incorrect because Ruth Benedict is associated with the Culture and Personality theory.

5. The correct answer is B. A symbol is something that represents something else. Choice A is incorrect because syntax refers to rules for constructing sentences. Choice C is incorrect because grammar refers to the rules of how a language is written and/ or spoken. Choice D is incorrect because phonology is the study of language sounds.

6. The correct answer is C. During the Neolithic era agriculture emerged: the deliberate production of food by growing crops and tending animals. Choice A is incorrect because the extinction of *Homo neanderthalensis* likely occurred prior to the emergence of agriculture. While the production of pottery, (choice B) occurred during the Neolithic era, it is not considered the defining feature of the Neolithic Revolution. Choice D is incorrect because the earliest expression of human imagination through cave art dates to the upper Paleolithic era.

7. The correct answer is D. Orangutans (found in Sumatra and Borneo) are generally solitary creatures who tend to forage for food over broad areas. Choices A, B, and C are incorrect because those primates tend to live in groups with others of their kind.

8. The correct answer is C. Anthropologists will often produce a written account of their time conducting fieldwork, complete with detailed descriptions of the culture they encountered and any patterns they may have observed. Choice A is incorrect because anthropologists prefer to participate in the everyday lives of people rather than in the controlled environment of a laboratory. Choice B is incorrect because an ethnography is a detailed description of a cultural group with more detail than a demographic list. Choice D is incorrect because an ethnography is usually an original work by one or more anthropologists written with a specific theoretical perspective.

9. **The correct answer is A.** Franz Boas's argument that cultures must be understood through the history that produced them is a direct critique of the idea that all cultures evolve through distinct states. Choice B is incorrect because the four forces of evolution is a concept from biology. Choice C is incorrect because Boas developed Historical Particularism decades before the emergence of neo-evolutionary thought. Choice D is incorrect because Boas was a supporter of cultural relativism, which argues that each culture must be understood by its own norms and values and not be immediately judged by the standards of other cultures.

10. **The correct answer is C.** Cultural determinism studies the role of culture in shaping a person's personality. Choice A is incorrect because the belief that one's own cultural norms are the only correct standard for living and should be used to judge others is referred to as ethnocentrism. Choice B is incorrect because cultural evolution argues that culture moves through the three stages of savagery, barbarism, and civilization. Choice D is incorrect because culture is not transmitted through genes. People learn and share culture through communication.

11. **The correct answer is D.** Anthropologists often observe cultures where the ideal set of behaviors and beliefs (ideal culture) is different from how people behave (real culture). Choice A is incorrect because culture itself is referred to as a system of symbols; these symbols are not necessarily related to norms and ideal behavior. Choice B is incorrect because adaptive and nonadaptive culture refers to behavior that helps people survive changes in the environment. Choice C is incorrect because "shared and learned" refer to characteristics of culture, not tensions with cultures.

12. **The correct answer is B.** Anthropologists focus on understanding the emic perspective: the point of view of the person who is part of that cultural group. Choice A is incorrect as that refers to the etic perspective: the point of view of someone who is outside of a cultural group. Choices C and D are incorrect as the emic perspective simply refers to the social position of the person (inside of a group), not their religious or secular perspective.

13. **The correct answer is B.** Foragers move from place to place as the seasons change, vegetation dies and grows, and animals move. Since foragers must carry all of their belonging as they move, they tend to have few material possessions. Choice A is incorrect because while foragers are focused on gathering fruits, vegetables, and plants, that does not completely negate their interest in owning material possessions. Choice C is incorrect because foragers do own personal material items. Choice D is incorrect because foragers use simple tools such as spears, digging sticks, and bows and arrows.

14. **The correct answer is A.** Choice A is correct because in unilateral (also known as unilineal) descent, descent is traced through either the patrilineal or matrilineal lines. Choice B is incorrect because bilateral descent is traced through both the paternal and maternal lines. Choice C is incorrect because a phratry is at least two clans who believe they are related to one another. Choice D is incorrect because a moiety refers to a society divided into two major descent groups; each half is referred to as a moiety. Each moiety usually consists of several clans.

15. **The correct answer is C.** *Open class* refers to stratified systems where there is a possibility of moving between the different levels of a social hierarchy. Choice A is incorrect because a society of relative equals is referred to as an egalitarian society. Choice B is incorrect because a society of chiefs and commoners is referred to as a rank society. Choice D is incorrect because stratified systems where there is no possibility of moving between the different levels of a social hierarchy is a closed class system.

16. **The correct answer is B.** Archaeologists are the experts at carefully recovering, cataloging, and studying items created and/or shaped by people, in this case a ship. Choice A is incorrect because physical anthropologists focus on the biological history and diversity of humanity. Choice C is incorrect because linguists study human language. Choice D is incorrect because cultural anthropologists focus on human cultural diversity.

17. **The correct answer is A.** A genotype refers to the genes and alleles each person possesses. Choice B is incorrect because one allele dominating the other refers to Mendel's principle of dominance. Choice C is incorrect because the four forces of evolution are mutation, genetic drift, gene flow, and natural selection. Choice D is incorrect because there is no official numeric classification system for fossils.

18. **The correct answer is B.** Paleoanthropologists have discovered fossil evidence that supports the idea that *Australopithecus afarensis* was likely the first human ancestor to walk on two legs. Choice A is incorrect because *Australopithecus afarensis* likely had apelike features. Choice C is incorrect because there is no evidence that *Australopithecus afarensis* invented the wheel or any other complicated tool. Choice D is incorrect because *Australopithecus afarensis* did not exist during the time of the dinosaurs.

19. **The correct answer is D.** During the Paleolithic era, humans survived by foraging: collecting plants, fishing, and hunting animals in order to survive. Choice A is incorrect because agriculture emerged during the Neolithic era. Choice B is incorrect because the animal domestication that is necessary for pastoralism emerged during the Neolithic era. Choice C is incorrect because the agricultural techniques of horticulturalists emerged during the Neolithic era.

20. **The correct answer is D.** Cultures change and innovate at their own pace. Decades of ethnographic research and cross-culture comparisons refute the idea that cultures evolve through the same stages over time. Choice A is incorrect because Morgan and Tylor did not conduct ethnographic fieldwork. They were considered armchair anthropologists because they never went into the field. Choice B is incorrect because industrialism was considered part of the civilization stage. Choice C is incorrect because Morgan and Tylor collected second- and third-hand information from around the world.

21. **The correct answer is A.** *Cultural universals* refer to something that is present in all cultures. Anthropologists debate about what counts as a universal and if they do, in fact, exist in all cultures. *Ethnology* refers to the practice of comparing and contrasting the cultural patterns of one group with other ethnographic examples. This could potentially reveal something present in every world culture. Choice B is incorrect because although observation is an anthropological method, it does not, by itself, provide the necessary cross-cultural comparison. Choice C is incorrect because interviewing as the only anthropological technique would not provide the necessary cross-cultural data to study cultural universals. Choice D refers to a method in paleoanthropology or archaeology for determining the age of a fossil or artifact.

22. **The correct answer is A.** The formalist position is based on economic assumptions that state all people are rational, logical scarce, all people will behave in a universal way: they will consider the costs, benefits, time, and energy required for an action, and they behave in a way that is the most beneficial to themselves. Choices B and D are incorrect because the group or family needs will not be placed above those of the individual. Choice C is incorrect because the formalist position assumes people behave logically and rationally.

23. **The correct answer is B.** The number of genders present in a cultural group varies. The Hijras of India are neither gender male or female and are referred to as "third gender." Therefore, choices A, C, and D are incorrect.

24. **The correct answer is D.** Primatology is the biological research and observation of nonhuman primates to shed light on human evolution. Choice A is incorrect because archaeologists and cultural anthropologists usually research foraging societies. Choice B is incorrect because paleoanthropologists typically catalog *Homo sapiens* fossils. Choice C is incorrect because primordial cell development would interest physical anthropologists specializing in human variation.

25. **The correct answer is B.** Some *Homo habilis* sites contain Old-
    owan stone tools, some of the earliest evidence of tool making.
    Choice A is incorrect because *Homo neanderthalensis* used
    Mousterian stone tools (the variety of objects such as hand axes
    and wooden spears found at various sites). Choice C is incorrect
    because there is no evidence that *Homo habilis* existed at the
    same time as *Homo sapiens*. Choice D is incorrect because inten-
    sive food production occurred during the Neolithic era. *Homo
    habilis* lived during the Lower Paleolithic era.

26. **The correct answer is B.** Marvin Harris's famous article "The
    Cultural Ecology of India's Sacred Cattle" argues for a theory of
    Ecological Materialism. Choice A is incorrect because Cognitive
    Anthropology focuses on categories and the human mind. Choice
    C is incorrect because Functionalism argues that cultural institu-
    tions function to fulfill basic human biological needs and support
    the workings of society. Choice D is incorrect because Sociobiol-
    ogy studies the relationship between culture and genetics.

27. **The correct answer is D.** *Diffusion* refers to new ideas, devices,
    and/or innovations spread from one culture to another through
    migration, colonization, etc. Choice A is incorrect because
    cultural evolution does not exist; each culture changes at its own
    rate. There is no blueprint or chart for when and how a cul-
    tural group might experience any change. Choice B is incorrect
    because culture contact can lead to more innovation as shared
    ideas or items are changed to suit the needs of a different cultural
    group. Choice C is incorrect because diffusion is about ideas that
    are not forgotten but are, in fact, exchanged and passed along to
    others.

28. **The correct answer is C.** Whether maintaining customs (tradi-
    tional behaviors) or punishing the violation of formal codes of
    conduct (laws), political organizations regulate behavior for social
    cohesion. Choice A is incorrect because invention and innova-
    tion are related to cultural change. Choice B is incorrect because
    foraging and agriculture are forms of subsistence strategy. Choice
    D is incorrect because participant observation and interviewing
    are anthropological research methods.

29. **The correct answer is C.** *Kinship* refers to a network of relatives related by blood or marriage. Choice A is incorrect because a lineage is a specific term referring to a unilineal kinship group descended from a common ancestor. Choice B is incorrect because maternal and paternal blood relatives are referred to as kindred. Choice D is incorrect because kinship terminology is defined as specific ways relatives are labeled or referred to.

30. **The correct answer is C.** Sacred narratives (also known as myths) are sacred stories that explain the relationship between the supernatural and reality. Choice A is incorrect because anthropologists do not categorize sacred narratives as true nor false. Choice B is incorrect because rituals invoking supernatural power to effect change refers to magic. Choice D is incorrect because a ritual that tries to discover hidden information or find lost people or objects is referred to as divination.

31. **The correct answer is C.** Archaeologists conduct cultural resource management: conserving material culture in accordance with laws for historic preservation. Choice A is incorrect because historical linguists are concerned with the connection between languages and how those languages change over time. Choice B is incorrect because paleoanthropologists reconstruct humanity's evolutionary past using the fossil record. Choice D is incorrect because ethnographers are usually cultural anthropologists who are researching and comparing patterns of human cultural diversity.

32. **The correct answer is C.** Rites of intensification bind a group together and reinforce the norms and values of that group. Choice A is incorrect because rites of passage are rituals that mark an individual's movement from one social status or stage of life to another. These include ceremonies for birth, marriage, aging, and death. Choice B is incorrect because rites of purification ritually cleanse a person or group when a taboo has been violated. Choice D is incorrect because syncretism occurs when two or more religions merge into a new faith.

33. **The correct answer is D.** *Closed class* refers to stratified systems where there is no possibility of moving between the different levels of a social hierarchy. In the closed class system, a person's location in the hierarchy is based on ascribed status: the position a person was born into. Choices A and B are incorrect because *monogamy* refers to having one spouse at a time, while *polygamy* refers to having multiple spouses at a time. Choice C is incorrect because *open class* refers to stratified systems where there is a possibility of moving between the different levels of a social hierarchy. In the open class system, where a person is located in the hierarchy is based on achieved status: what a person is able to accomplish through their own actions.

34. **The correct answer is C.** Division of labor refers to cultural groups deciding which person or group will be responsible for completing particular tasks. Choice A is incorrect because the time spent working is not necessarily related to division of labor. Choice B is incorrect because not all work is salaried. Choice D is incorrect because division of labor refers to categories of workers, not a set of tasks.

35. **The correct answer is A.** In response to great social changes and high levels of stress or unhappiness, revitalization movements may emerge. These movements promise widespread reforms, based on religious beliefs, which will improve life and end suffering. Some movements are messianic, believing that an individual will change the world into paradise. Choice B is incorrect because a millenarian movement believes that a catastrophe will destroy most of the world but will eventually lead to heaven on earth. Choice C is incorrect because a totemic religious movement believes ancestral spirits bind them together as one people and, as a result, they have a special relationship with an animal, plant, or other object that represents that spirit. Choice D is incorrect because secularization is when a society moves away from a religious worldview.

36. **The correct answer is C.** Anthropologists will often conduct cross-cultural comparisons of observed patterns to determine if there are any significant parallels between cultural groups. This is called ethnology. Choice A is incorrect because ethnographer refers to the anthropologist conducting the study. Choice B is incorrect because an ethnography is the detailed written description of a cultural group. Choice D is incorrect because ethnomusicology is the study of the relationship between music and culture.

37. **The correct answer is B.** Magic, divination, and sacrifice are examples of rituals, ceremonial acts designed for use during specific occasions. Choice A is incorrect because myths are sacred stories that explain the relationship between the supernatural and reality. Choice C is incorrect because exogamy is when an individual must marry outside his or her own group. Choice D is incorrect because reciprocity is when people exchange goods and services that are of roughly equal value.

38. **The correct answer is C.** All over the world, as culture change continues and globalization tightens connections between people and places, indigenous groups fight for cultural survival: the right to preserve, remember, and celebrate one's culture. Choice A is incorrect because a cultural universal is something that is found in every culture. Choice B is incorrect because artifacts from early human cultures are also referred to as material culture or cultural remains. Choice D is incorrect because cultures can be preserved in ways other than historical records, for example, art, literature, and multimedia.

39. **The correct answer is C.** Historical linguists are concerned with the connection between languages and how these languages change over time. Choice A is incorrect because structural linguists are focused on how a language is constructed (grammar, syntax, etc.). Choice B is incorrect because cultural anthropologists focus on cultural patterns of human behavior. Choice D is incorrect because historic archaeologists analyze both cultural artifacts and written evidence to understand a group of people.

40. **The correct answer is C.** Paleoanthropologists have discovered fossil evidence that *Homo erectus* was likely producing Acheulean stone tools, oval-shaped hand tools. Choice A is incorrect because *Australopithecus afarensis* likely used tools like a modern chimpanzee. Choice B is incorrect because *Homo habilis* is associated with Oldowan stone tools: rocks were shaped by striking flakes off. *Homo neanderthalensis* (choice D) is incorrect because they are associated with Mousterian stone tools: the variety of objects such as hand axes and wooden spears found at various sites.

41. **The correct answer is D.** Animism is the belief that everything is made of spirits or supernatural energies. Choice A is incorrect because sacrifice is an offering to supernatural beings to demonstrate faith and loyalty. Choice B is incorrect because witchcraft refers to magical rituals used to cause harm. Choice C is incorrect because syncretism is the merging of two or more religions into a new faith.

42. **The correct answer is C.** Sociolinguists study language use by different groups in various social contexts. Choices B and D are incorrect because descriptive and structural linguists refer to people who study the construction of languages. Choice A is incorrect because historical linguists are concerned with the connection between languages and how these languages change over time.

43. **The correct answer is C.** Gorilla social behavior, skeleton structure, and eating habits all give primatologists clues as to how humans may have evolved over time. Choice A is incorrect because chimpanzee DNA is 98 percent the same as human DNA. Choice B is incorrect because orangutans have been observed catching termites with branches and attempting to spear fish out of rivers. Choice D is incorrect because meerkats are not primates.

44. **The correct answer is C.** Boas and Malinowski practiced and taught their students participant observation: spending an extended period of time with a group of people observing, interviewing, and participating in the activities of their everyday lives. Choices A and B are incorrect because absolute and relative dating methods are used to determine the age of fossils or artifacts. Choice D is incorrect because armchair anthropology refers to reading accounts about other cultures (from explorers, missionaries, reporters, historians, etc.) and drawing conclusions based on that information—the opposite of participant observation.

45. **The correct answer is A.** Culture is best described as a set of behavioral patterns, norms, and values shared by a group. Choice B is incorrect because a cultural group may live in many territories. A single territory may have many cultural groups. Choices C and D are incorrect because, from an anthropological perspective, culture is shared individual's personality or belief system.

46. **The correct answer is D.** Redistribution occurs when goods are collected by a central person or office and then reallocated into the society. In industrialized state societies, for example, a government collects taxes and returns them to the populace in the form of national healthcare, education, etc. Choice A is incorrect because production refers to how resources are transformed into specific goods and services. Choice B is incorrect because a market exchange refers to the buying and selling of goods depending on supply and demand. Choice C is incorrect because people engage in reciprocity when they exchange goods and services that are of roughly equal value.

47. **The correct answer is A.** Agriculture allowed people to settle in one place and, over time, begin growing enough food to sustain larger and larger populations. Anthropological evidence suggests no large scale society has ever organized itself without social stratification (unequal access to resources). Choice B is incorrect because tool use emerged prior to large populations of human settlement. Choice C is incorrect because cave art dates back to the Upper Paleolithic era, likely prior to agriculture. Choice D is incorrect because people were moving from one place to another prior to the late Neolithic era.

48. **The correct answer is A.** Relative dating methods can only tell us if a fossil is older or younger than another fossil. Stratigraphy is one example of a relative dating method. Generally, deeper layers of dirt and rock are older than the surface layer of dirt. Choices B, C, and D are all examples of absolute dating and give us the age of something in actual years.

49. **The correct answer is C.** Evidence suggests that cave art was likely produced by *Homo sapiens* over 30,000 years ago, what archaeologists refer to as the Upper Paleolithic era. Choices A and B are incorrect because the Lower and Middle Paleolithic eras occurred before the Upper Paleolithic era. Choice D is incorrect because the Neolithic era occurred after the Upper Paleolithic era.

50. **The correct answer is D.** Physical anthropologists often use their skills to conduct forensic anthropology, the analysis of skeletal remains. These remains may be part of an FBI or police investigation, and careful examination can provide the clues necessary to help solve a case. Choice A is incorrect because primatologists study nonhuman primates to shed light on human evolution. Choice B is incorrect because cultural anthropologists focus on researching and comparing patterns of human cultural diversity. Choice C is incorrect because linguists study human language.

51. **The correct answer is D.** A pilgrimage refers to traveling to a sacred site to prove one's dedication to the faith. Choice A is incorrect because a religious movement that promises widespread reform is a revitalization movement. Choice B is incorrect because traveling for tourism is simply tourism. Choice C is incorrect because migrating to a new country is known as immigrating.

52. **The correct answer is D.** Cultural anthropologists focus on researching and comparing patterns of human cultural diversity through participant observation. Choice A is incorrect because maritime archaeologists search for artifacts in bodies of water. Choice B is incorrect because primatologists study nonhuman primates to shed light on human evolution. Choice C is incorrect because forensic anthropologists analyze skeletal remains.

53. **The correct answer is D.** The phenotype refers to the physical expression of the genotype. A person may have inherited alleles for dark (for example, black) and light (for example, blond) hair from their parents. Choices A, B, and C are incorrect because an allele is a group of genes located on sections of DNA that can only be seen at the microscopic level.

54. **The correct answer is A.** Elites (governments, for example) historically have been the cause of directed culture change: when those with power (often the people at the top of a socially stratified society) develop and enforce plans that force the less powerful to accept changes. Choice B is incorrect because there are no forces of cultural evolution. Choice C is incorrect because directed cultural change is not related to witchcraft. Choice D is incorrect because totemism is evidence of people having a special relationship with an animal, plant, or other object that represents ancestral spirits.

55. **The correct answer is B.** Political associations refer to the categories of bands, tribes, chiefdoms, or states; these are the ways cultural groups organize themselves to maintain social order. Choice A is incorrect because voter organization is one of the many ways of maintaining social order. Choice C is incorrect because the Neolithic Revolution occurred over a long period of time and was not a product of political associations. Choice D is incorrect because the formalist and substantivist debate was a theoretical debate, not an actual one.

56. **The correct answer is D.** During the Neolithic era, humans began guiding the growth of plants and the reproduction of animals. Choices A, B, and C are incorrect because none of these answers is directly connected to agriculture or the care of livestock.

57. **The correct answer is D.** Individuals who have traits that allow them to survive and reproduce are said to be better adapted to the environment they live in. Choices A and B are incorrect because successful adaptation means passing on the traits that helped the individual survive—reproduction. Choice C is incorrect because preparation for natural disasters is less directly related to reproduction.

58. **The correct answer is C.** Cultural relativism argues that each culture must be understood by its own norms and values and not be immediately judged by the standards of other cultures. This perspective has its roots in the work of Franz Boas and many of his students. Their work is collectively referred to as historical particularism. Choices A, B, and D are incorrect as those are all theoretical frameworks that emerged after historical particularism.

59. **The correct answer is A.** *Neolocal* refers to spouses living separately from their parents in their own households. Choices B and D are incorrect because *bilocal* and *ambilocal* refer to spouses choosing which family to live with or near. Choice C is incorrect because *avunculocal* refers to spouses living with or near the husband's mother's brother.

60. **The correct answer is D.** Elites (governments, for example) historically have been the cause of directed culture change: when those with power (often the people at the top of a socially stratified society) develop and enforce plans that force the less powerful to accept changes. Choice A is incorrect because random changes in DNA that may lead to beneficial, harmful, or neutral traits for an organism are referred to as mutation. Choice B is incorrect because an event such as an earthquake that causes an individual to die without reproducing is referred to as genetic drift. Choice C is incorrect because understanding how different cultural components work with one another is referred to as holism or the holistic perspective.

Printed in the USA
CPSIA information can be obtained
at www.ICGtesting.com
JSHW012043140824
68134JS00033B/3237